CONCILIUM

THEOLOGY IN THE AGE OF RENEWAL

CONCILIUM

CONCILIUM/VOL. 32

LITURGY

REFORMING THE RITES OF DEATH

edited by JOHANNES WAGNER

VOLUME 32

CONCILIUM
theology in the age of renewal

PAULIST PRESS
NEW YORK, N.Y. / GLEN ROCK, N.J.

The Imprimatur for this volume applies
only to articles by Roman Catholic authors.

NIHIL OBSTAT: John E. Brooks, S.J., S.T.D.
Censor Deputatus

IMPRIMATUR: ✠ Bernard J. Flanagan, D.D.
Bishop of Worcester

January 31, 1968

The Nihil Obstat and Imprimatur are official declarations that a book or
pamphlet is free of doctrinal or moral error. No implication is contained
therein that those who have granted the Nihil Obstat and Imprimatur agree
with the contents, opinions or statements expressed.

Library of Congress Catalogue Card Number: 68-20845

Suggested Decimal Classification: 264.02

Paulist Press assumes responsibility for the accuracy of the English translations in this Volume.

PAULIST PRESS
EXECUTIVE OFFICES: 304 W. 58th Street, New York, N.Y. and 21 Harris-
town Road, Glen Rock, N.J.
Executive Publisher: John A. Carr, C.S.P.
Executive Manager: Alvin A. Illig, C.S.P.
Asst. Executive Manager: Thomas E. Comber, C.S.P.

EDITORIAL OFFICES: 304 W. 58th Street, New York, N.Y.
Editor: Kevin A. Lynch, C.S.P.
Managing Editor: Urban P. Intondi

Printed and bound in the United States of America by
The Colonial Press Inc., Clinton, Mass.

CONTENTS

PART II

BIBLIOGRAPHICAL SURVEY

PART III

DOCUMENTATION CONCILIUM
Office of the Executive Secretary
Nijmegen, Netherlands

PREFACE

Heinrich Rennings / *Trier, W. Germany*

The *Constitution on the Sacred Liturgy* of Vatican Council II has demanded a reform of the present burial rite. What shape should the new liturgical regulations take in order to suit the Christian community at the departure of one of its members? First of all, such liturgical gatherings should follow the lines laid down for the whole renewal of the liturgy: active participation, a more interesting use of the Bible, intelligibility of the symbols, etc. To this the Constitution adds a special note for the burial rite when it says that it "should express more clearly the paschal character of Christian death" (n. 81).

On the basis of this document Work-group 23 of the Consilium for the implementation of the *Constitution on the Sacred Liturgy* has worked out a project for the burial of an adult which has been tried out in many places throughout the world since the summer of 1966. When this experimental period comes to an end and the reports on the frequently useful practical results of the experiment have been assimilated, this project will become the model burial rite in the *Rituale Romanum*. This means that it will be the basis for the burial rites adopted in the regional Rituals which must be worked out by the Episcopal Conferences according to article 63b of the Constitution.

When the work on the model rite for the Roman Ritual is

1

finished, the reform of the funeral liturgy will not yet therefore come to an end; rather, it will be the beginning of a new phase, namely, that of the ensuing adaptation of this model rite to regional requirements and situations under the guidance of the Episcopal Conferences. This adaptation can certainly not be limited to a vernacular translation of the texts of the Roman Ritual. Nor will it be enough simply to make a choice from the possible variations provided in the model rite. It would be asking too much of this rite to demand that it provide answers for every possible requirement.

The elaboration of local burial rites within the jurisdiction of the Episcopal Conferences (and taking into account the differences of language) raises a number of questions, some of which this present volume proposes to deal with.

If the burial rite must proclaim the paschal meaning of a Christian death in word and sign, one cannot avoid some consideration of the anthropological presuppositions of such a proclamation. What does modern man—or more accurately— what do people of a given culture think of death? To find out about the situation of those to whom this proclamation is addressed, we can begin with an analysis of prevalent tendencies in philosophy, literature, the plastic arts, sociology and psychology. What kind of notion of death lies behind the concrete forms a burial takes outside the Christian community. Has this any meaning for the Christian burial?

Another necessary condition for a new burial rite is some consideration of the theological content of what the Christian message has to say about dying, death and "the last things" in general. For instance, is the description of death as a "separation of body and soul" satisfactory or misleading? Should this manner of speaking still occur in the prayers? How should the liturgical texts express such realities of the faith as purgatory, heaven, hell, last judgment, resurrection, beatific vision, new heaven, new earth and others? Not merely in a way that is intelligible to people today and takes their prejudices into account, but so as to ensure that these realities appear to them for what they are:

the unexpected fulfillment of their secret longings and a God-given certainty beyond all their guessing. One cannot expect prayers of the early Middle Ages to appeal to the modern Christian's understanding of creation and the world. That is why texts taken from ancient sources cannot by themselves provide a new liturgy. The fact that there are truths about dying, death and resurrection, which mean little or nothing to many people, forces us at least not to make the Christian message still more unintelligible by the use of unrealistic words and phrases about the revelation.

A new funeral liturgy must be sufficiently elastic in detail and in its overall cohesion not to clamp fixed forms on varying circumstances so that rite and burial can become an organic unity. The liturgical arrangements must therefore take note of the nature and various kinds of burial, such as the ceremonial lying in the coffin at home, in a public funeral parlor or some other place; interment or cremation, or burial at sea. Other differences derive from the composition of the congregation present: a small group of relatives, mainly non-Christian mourners, a whole tribe or whole village, a State funeral with numerous guests, and so on. Such differences in the attending congregation may well decide whether congregational singing is possible or not. It would be a mistake to make singing so important that, without singing, only the bare bones of a rite would remain (perhaps in the form of some recitation of a text that should be sung). Finally, the rite will also vary according to whether it is conducted by a bishop, a priest, a deacon or a layman.

We must also include in this discussion the question of a Mass celebrated at a funeral. How should that fit in with the other funeral ceremonies? Before? After? At a different time? What form should such a eucharistic gathering take in regard to the death of a Christian? The need to reform the text and rites of the "Requiem Mass" is obvious. Is there a chance to celebrate the Mass within the family circle instead of in a vast empty church if there are only a few mourners?

For a renewal of the funeral liturgy, it would also be useful

for the Church of Rome to investigate other Christian rites in
other Churches: non-Roman Latin liturgies, the burial service in
the Eastern Churches, the Reformed Churches and other Christian denominations. Because of its size this volume can only deal
with this by way of a few examples.

Everything connected with a burial must reflect the fact that
a Christian's death is a sharing in the paschal death and resurrection of the Lord. From a multitude of customs only a few
questions are chosen connected with the resting place of a dead
Christian. The age of "God's acre", the plot of land around the
Church, "God's House", is gone. The "confessional" cemetery
is becoming the exception: if Christians strive after unity in life,
why separate them in death? The living Christian who has spent
his life among non-believers, sharing in a common human destiny, will also find his grave among them. Why should not his
grave bear witness to his faith, just as his life did?

PART I
ARTICLES

Wilhelm Breuning/*Trier, W. Germany*

Death and Resurrection in the Christian Message

Concilium, Vol. 26, 1967, had a Documentation section on "Death and Afterlife". This showed that, if one looks for it, there is more in the general uncertainty about eschatological issues than meets the eye. I refer to this article because I am taking it as the basis for this present article. It saves me from having to wade through contemporary literature for the sake of mere information. The information there given suits our purpose the better for grouping the various approaches to the problem into three typical categories: the apocalyptic approach, the teleological expectation of the future and the prophetic approach. In what follows, I am not concerned with a comparative study of these three types, but rather with the question of what possibilities the combination of all three offer to the preacher who is called upon to speak somewhat meaningfully about the content of the kind of hope that not only gives some real sense to Christian life but presents us also with a credible theodicy. The complex nature of such an investigation cannot be dealt with here in detail; I can only indicate some general lines, conveniently drawn together as for a thesis. For the literature referring to particular questions I refer to that Documentation section already mentioned above.

I

The Theological Structure of an Eschatological Statement

It is generally agreed that a statement of faith is replete with difficulties where eschatology is concerned. This is why there is in eschatology such a gap between what is really meant and what can be expressed in words that anything may happen in between. This gap, which allows full play to so many factors, shows more particularly how the notions in use are obscured by being conveyed in particularly unsuitable presentations that belong to a naive, scientifically, out-of-date image of the world. This is the image that, in the past, has wrapped up the specific character of a given situation in the peculiar framework in which it took place.

As a statement of fact this is so generally accepted that it needs no further explanation. But we do need to give some thought to the value of this fact. Are we wrong when we think that these obscurities lead mainly to a negative attitude? They certainly make it very difficult today to say something significant about death and resurrection. On the other hand, we might look again at the "real meaning" and the "formulation in words" to see whether these two elements do not contain possibilities that might be useful in our proclamation of the truth. The admission that there is such a wide gap between what is really meant and what can be expressed in words is basically a sign that theological thought is on the right track. And the critical standards to which we subject our presentation are surely a help in trying to measure the gap. For it is not the task of theology to relieve the tension between the two but rather to keep it alive. We must now try to apply this in a concrete way to our topic.

(a) In technical theological terminology we express the existence of this gap, this tension, by saying that our theological statements must be interpreted "analogically". This does not diminish the conviction that God himself is truly involved in our statement: he is involved as a reality in our statement, and therefore precisely as mystery. Of course, God's reality is not involved in a sentence if we take this as a purely abstract sentence. But every sentence is only meaningful when spoken by man. And insofar as God's saving mystery is concerned, we can only speak in the language of faith. This language of faith turns any complete statement *about* God into words that are directly pointing *toward* God. Only then do we speak rightly "about God". In every statement of faith the word directed toward God is man's surrender to the God who is always "greater", the *Deus semper maior,* whose greatness is experienced as present precisely because it leads man into the mystery that is constantly greater than we thought. An analogous statement about God means therefore that when we make an essentially relevant statement about God we can do so only in a language that is understood on the basis of faith, hope and charity. If we keep this in mind, every statement of faith "understands" God really in that he wants to *share* himself as the *mystery* of infinite love in precisely this always surpassing greatness of his. Only in this context can statements of faith have any meaning at all. This preserves the theocentrism that draws man toward this mystery and away from himself. It also preserves the anthropocentrism of God, who meets man in the totality of his mystery. Eschatological statements offer, so to speak, a classical instance of this analogy, which we find throughout the whole field of revelation theology. They can only have meaning within this personal relationship. On the side of God, their content is the finality of God's loving commitment to man. On the side of man, they always imply that when man has reached fulfillment he has "understood" this finality of God insofar as he is concerned. If man says something about it at present, he always speaks in anticipation. This anticipation does not primarily relate to man's final fate but is rather the basic condition from which he must proceed whenever and wherever he meets God in faith. In other words, an eschatological statement has the same certainty, intensity and concrete meaning as any statement about God. But it has, to the same extent, that openness which always points to the greater reality beyond. Nevertheless, it never excludes man as part of a purely earthly future because such a statement implies the presence of a God who makes himself available to man.

(b) Given these characteristic features of eschatological statements, we must necessarily have a discerning attitude toward the content of these statements. Such an attitude is based on the statements of the revelation and has been put to use deliberately in what is called the "negative theology" (the theology that works out what God is not). And he who is very keen on purifying eschatological statements from the influence of primitive images of the world, would be simply forcing an open door. He might even overlook the fact that the statements of revelation and their deposit in Scripture have already done this in a far more thorough way than it has been done by scientific criticism of that primitive world image. But this does not mean that such constructive criticism or discernment can be found in every scriptural statement and at the same level. Nor is it a simple datum but rather a repercussion that comes from being in touch with the reality of the eschatological mystery itself.

If we look at an example like chapter 21 of the Apocalypse —one among many possible examples—it becomes clear that the eschatological quality (the "newness") does not come from heavenly space, but that this space receives its quality from God. (One should, in this respect, have a good look at what is said about God and the Lamb as Temple and Light of the eschatological City in 5, 22–4.) In an edition of the Bible where the text is accompanied with cross references to the Old Testament one can see how often the corresponding Old Testament texts are essentially and ultimately concerned with the presence of God. That the biblical authors shared a pre-scientific image of the world is hardly astonishing and therefore not a source of worry. But while seeing this, one should not overlook that underlying deeper criticism of the old image made in those texts: they show that the quality of the eschatological reality does not derive from those conceptions of this world but from God. In other words, the reality of the world does not vanish before God but is rather seen as created by God and deriving its value from this fact. It is therefore of the essence of an eschatological statement that the created reality is seen as related to God, but in such a way that the expression of this relationship is always critically aware of the tension between the boundless hope that flows from the knowledge of a God who always exceeds our understanding and the impossibility to express this boundlessness otherwise than as a *pointer* toward this hope.

When we begin with this necessary critical awareness, which is the basic feature of all negative theology, it will hardly astonish us that this tension is more easily brought out by way of images than through notions. The Bible and the liturgy of the dead contain a rich fund of such images which should not first be demythologized because, operating at the higher level of a negative theology concerned with the mystery of God, it is beyond simple scientific criticism. The critical approach, so often met with today, seems only to lead to what can no longer be said, what does not longer quite "fit" and therefore must be dropped, and consequently seems to give the impression that we can constantly say less, thus paying for our rational criticism with an inevitable shrinking of the content of our belief. On the other hand, negative theology with its criticism derived from within revelation can express what only the hope in the *Deus semper maior* can express.

We may broadly sum up what has been said as follows: although eschatology is mainly concerned with man's ultimate fate, the basic presupposition is that the statements concerning man are theocentric. At the root of it all we have to explain what is contained in every statement about God, namely, that no right statement about God can ever be neutral insofar as man is concerned. An eschatological statement simply brings out this implication more intensively and more urgently.

II

THE FACE OF UNREDEEMED DEATH

The context of personal theism does not only hold for man's final state but also for his dying.

(a) First of all, dying here becomes a process which is not only limited to man's body but also involves man as a whole. Contemporary man does not find it difficult to accept this way of looking at it. The idealistic view that the immortal soul is not affected by the process of dying, and even comes into its own spiritually, is rejected by many today. When, in the face of his own death or that of one of his loved ones, one tries to console him with talk of the "immortal" soul, he reacts with mistrust. To be satisfied with the definition of death as separation of body and soul means that one presupposes a certain idealizing notion of the soul which takes for granted that the soul happily continues to exist by itself. In that case death may be very unpleasant and full of sorrow and cause understandable anxiety, but in fact it does not really touch the essence of the person.

The entry of idealizing tendencies into the Christian view of death was primarily due to the related concept of judgment. Judgment is clearly a process that affects the whole man. The danger in spiritualizing one's concept of death then came to rest in the resultant absence of any interior connection between the separation of body and soul on the one hand and the judgment on the other.

But in the context of revelation, man's whole existence is threatened by death. Man experiences this threat not merely as something dark, indefinite and uncertain but he sees that at the root this threat lies in his existence before God. The more man lives in the face of God, the more deeply will he experience this threat of death.

(b) This total view of death does not come any closer by simply eliminating the doctrine of "immortality". One may rightly wonder whether the term "immortality" is the happiest expression of what is really meant. This expression may raise two objections in one's mind: first, the wrong idea that the soul is not touched by death, and secondly, the wrong idea that immortality is a kind of chemical quality inherent in the spirit. What is really meant could not be more gravely misinterpreted than by seeing in the spirit's relation to eternity a kind of physical quality. But although it is right to criticize such a metaphysics as too "physical", one should not overlook the fact that the personal spirit has as its attribute a kind of irrevocability before God that cannot just dissolve into nothing through death. It is precisely this irrevocability that makes it impossible to look for a right understanding of death in the separation of body and soul and the preservation of the soul. In our context we should rather conceive of death as something that involves the person of God and the person of man.

(c) This context makes it plain, however, that the statement concerning the irrevocability of the person before God provides no security against death, but rather reveals the most threatening aspect of death to its full extent. It is common human experience that no one's life can be safe from death. This implies more than the mere fact that death can come at any moment and quite suddenly. On this side of death, the really bitter taste lies rather in our awareness of the defective validity of every human life in the depth of our unquenchable thirst for our own validity and that of all we love. To have this basic feeling one need not have passed through a complete life. The element of doubt which besets even all our good deeds is enough to become aware of this threat to life. Within the context of revelation this experience becomes a certainty and grief, that no man has any "standing" before God. (There is no need to insert here the whole doctrine of sin, which really is a partial theological analysis of this "being without standing".) In the light of revelation this futility of man, made plain in death, stands out even more sharply through the knowledge that it is made everlasting through and in death. Seen from the human angle, death leaves no room for a possible, ultimate escape, but, without God, throws man back irrevocably on that fragment of himself now cut off from life. One may wonder whether the Old Testament notion of a shadow existence for those that have died could not still be helpful in understanding this situation insofar as that notion would supply a more truthful and correct picture than the idealistic illusion that sees in death a kind of deliverance.

(d) In view of the seriousness with which Scripture speaks of death as "non-salvation" (*Unheil*) incarnate, we also have to state that, humanly speaking, we cannot see death as a deed of man. In death man finalizes his inability to dispose of himself in love. Death in the state of "non-salvation" has the character of a breakdown which man himself cannot mend.

III

THE DEATH OF THE REDEEMER

The sharp insight, without illusion, into the negative character of death is brought out, within the scope of the Christian message, not as an isolated theology of non-salvation, but rather and only in the knowledge of Christ's death as the death that brings salvation. This knowledge is not a mere variation in the process of how to assess death but the very heart of the Christian message of salvation. The positive view of Christ's death as a saving death presupposes the understanding of the negative character of death. Christ died the death of sin (cf. Rom. 8, 3). The deepening of the eschatological statement about death presupposes here, above all, a deepening of our soteriology (theology of redemption). Christ not only assumes the biological process of the disintegration of senses and body in the particularly agonizing form of punishment but shares the whole situation of death with us. He whose life was surrender of himself for the sake of others, intentionally and effectively had inevitably to face the end of his life before his self-giving love had reached its goal and so its fulfillment. The coercion that breaks all other men in one way or another, became in his case the vessel of a love, unmarred for all its tenderness, which flowed from the death-wound of this life. But this would again lead to a crowing about man's ability to overcome death himself if we overlooked the fact that the fruitfulness of this self-giving death was due to something that happened at a personal level between Jesus and his Father. This encounter has two facets. From the point of view of Jesus it is the adoring self-surrender to the mystery of the Father. From the point of view of the Father it is the final self-communication of God in all his glory which is poured into the loving self-emptying of the Son. (That the trinitarian relationship is here realized in the human life of Christ should be stressed particularly, but there is no room to develop this here.)

IV

THE RESURRECTION AS A CHRIST-HAPPENING

It is precisely this personal consideration of Christ's death which leads us inevitably to a further conclusion, namely, that the death and resurrection of Jesus must be seen as far more closely intertwined than is still frequently the case. The theology of the liturgy has essentially contributed to a re-discovery of the unity of the paschal mystery. But it is very important that this unity is not conceived as an afterthought to the interpretation of what happened, but rather as a believing insight into the mystery itself. We should not see here merely possible solutions for too superficial apologetics but rather the key that opens all the doors in the whole problem of our eschatology.[1]

(a) Resurrection, too, is first of all a personal happening between Christ and the Father. Only in this perspective can one speak meaningfully about resurrection.

(b) Resurrection does not explain away death but it is God's answer to man's death in sin, which God did not will.[2] Insofar as this answer is a creative act of God, which he alone is able to posit, it re-creates from within the negative power of death that must be overcome. Through the final grace of God even death becomes the instrument of adoration and life for the many. Thus death can become what, without the Son of love, it never was and could never become, namely, a passage, a transit, and not the sealing off of a fragmentary existence. This passage or

---

[1] What follows holds primarily for the resurrection of Christ. But for a large part the same views are important for understanding our own resurrection.

[2] This description refers to the character of death as analyzed above.

transit, however, does not lead into another space which would, like another room in a house, be contiguous with the room of our earthly existence. It is rather the fullness of the mystery of God, which constantly strengthened the pilgrim on his way before he reached the passage. If, then, death meant for Christ a passage, it means that he has finally and absolutely "arrived" at the Father's mystery.

(c) If we think along the lines of revelation, it is impossible that God would only partially save the man Jesus whom he loved. God leads the whole man through the passage of death. The impossibility to find out how this comes about yields here to the absolute certainty that God loves the whole man and the consequent certainty that for God nothing of this man is lost.

Only a personalist understanding of the resurrection of the body can save us from unsatisfactory presentations and at the same time give us a deeper understanding of the reality of the body. God loves more than the molecules that happen to be present in the body at the moment of death. He loves a body that is marked by all the labor and all the longing of a pilgrimage, and which in the course of this pilgrimage has left many traces in a world that has become more human because of those traces; a body that has constantly absorbed the fullness of this world in order that man should not be without strength and without trace in this world; a body that has been hurt by the angularity of this world and is covered with scars and has yet continually and gently stretched out its arms toward this world. Resurrection of the body means that of all this nothing is lost where God is concerned because he loves man. All the tears have been gathered and no smile has been allowed to slip away unnoticed. Resurrection of the body means that man does not find in God only his last moments, but his whole story. It is not for nothing that in some narratives of the resurrection the risen Christ is said to bear the marks of his wounds, or that the letter to the Hebrews makes the high priest enter into the sanctuary with his blood (9, 12), or that the Apocalypse makes the Lamb live before the throne of God, as the slaughtered Lamb (5, 6).

(d) The confession of the resurrection of the body, therefore, says also something significant about the personalist meaning of the world. The bodily condition derives its whole meaning from the mutual attraction that reigns between man and world. The body is the bridge that has its foundation in both. The body is man insofar as with his whole being, including his relationship toward God and fellowman, he stands in the world and in this way lifts the world itself into the sphere of personal existence. When God decided in favor of man's resurrection, he implied the world with which man's bodily condition is related. But, then, this world must be a meaningful world, therefore a humanized world, as molded by man, the beloved of God.

(e) The manner of the risen bodily condition is still beyond our understanding. This is not a convenient excuse; nor is it a blind leap into the absurd. Many of the objections to the resurrection of Christ and to resurrection in general derive their conscious or unconscious strength mainly from the fact that resurrection is seen as a kind of "re-play" of life before death, and then one does not know what the whole thing really means: one has a body but one does not quite see what one can do with it. And so this body is, by some lasting miracle, maintained in some kind of spiritualized fool's paradise. I have tried to show that, from the personalist angle of a loving God, resurrection is not only meaningful but also a straightforward consequence of the seriousness of his love. Insofar as God's love is what we are most certain about in our faith (cf. Rom. 8, 31–9), we are related to this love through the hope of things not seen (cf. Heb. 11, 1). Our hope is in no sense a weakening of our faith in the love of God, nor is it a weakening when we admit our inability to pigeonhole the manner of our risen bodily condition in a way that would run ahead of our fulfillment. If I have stressed that God in his love lets nothing of us get lost, we are already faced with the impossibility to say in what this "wholeness" of ourselves consists in God's eyes. On the other hand, it is not difficult to see that the bodily condition after death—therefore, after having passed beyond death into the light of God's mystery—must entail some new kind of aggregate condition, particularly when it concerns ourselves. This theological attempt at explanation we find already in 1 Corinthians 15, 35–8. For the rest, this aggregate condition has nothing to do with the fool's paradise mentality I mentioned above, but rather with the observation at the beginning that it is God himself who determines the quality of the eschatological condition in his mystery.

If occasionally we nevertheless fall victim to our fairy-land presentation, the fault lies in our wooden theology of the *pneuma* (spirit). Resurrection—and particularly the resurrection of Jesus —takes place in the Spirit because it is above all a personal event that happens between Father and Son, and lets Father and Son live as a personal unity, therefore as a "community". In the resurrection of Christ the Spirit, being love, preserves the human mystery of Jesus by transfiguring it in the mystery of the Father and so allowing it to be one with the Son's eternal orientation toward the Father. If one has even a little pneumatological "imagination", one is familiar with the thought that the Spirit preserves while transforming and that he does not plunge man into self-alienation when he fills him with God. In any case Scripture sees in the resurrection a trinitarian process where the Spirit is the principle, not only of the momentary act of raising, but also of the living existence of the risen man in God (cf. Rom. 8, 10f.).[3]

V

CHRIST'S DEATH AND RESURRECTION AND OUR OWN

By linking our own resurrection so closely with that of Christ, we have run ahead of our explanation. There is still much to

---

[3] One may certainly wonder whether a "dispensation" theology of the beatific vision based on that of the Spirit would not help to overcome the weaknesses inherent in this theology. It is not so much a matter of an admiring contemplation of God's essence (which is here really mainly seen as Unity), but of being brought also into the depth of God as explored in 1 Corinthians 2, 10. There still remains the Spirit who reaches us from the glorified bodily condition of Jesus.

add about our connection with Christ's death if we wish to understand our own eschatological fate. We have looked at Christ's resurrection as one with his death. But we still have to see how his death changes ours.

(a) We start with the point that Christ's death can change the negative character of our common human death. But it is difficult to describe this change in such a way as to bring out the position of Christ with sufficient clarity. Many theories today tend to hold that it is not important to believe *in* Jesus but to believe *as* Jesus believed. Without denying the second point, I would prefer to make the possibility of believing *like* Jesus depend on belief *in* Jesus. In similar fashion there are many current presentations about the death of the faithful which bypass the issue. These seem to suggest that Jesus had but to demonstrate how we can get through the straits of death by turning death into an action. In that case Christ would be but the discoverer of a new "law" of salvation, which we must learn how to operate. It is, of course, not denied that the Christian should die as Jesus died. But this action does not consist in that he makes his own death his own action, but rather in that he makes Jesus' death his own. No positive transformation of death can put aside the presupposition that death is, first of all, the opposite of an action in the sense of man's disposal of himself by his own decision. The "non-salvation" (*Unheils-*) character of death is precisely the impossibility to turn it into a disposal of oneself that can stand up to God in its own right. Only one single death escaped from this law, and this could happen, as described above, because death was conquered from within through a personal deed. But in doing this, Christ did not just point the way which anyone can imitate: it can only be done through being personally "included" in Jesus. The transformation of death does, therefore, not take place by Jesus demonstrating how, against all appearances, we can nevertheless ourselves make something positive of death, but in the straightforward confession that there is only hope for our death in Jesus' self-surrender unto death.

The "for us" of Jesus' death is more than a demythologizing of naïve images of the primitive sacrifice and satisfaction—indeed it demands this demythologization. It is rooted in the conviction that, by letting us partake in his death, Jesus did not give us a moving but ultimately powerless altruistic impulse, but rather that in his love he embraced the anguish of death of all men within his own death. This love is not helpless and merely "well-meant" but has really penetrated there where all men are left alone with themselves in that "non-saving" way and where this "non-salvation" lies precisely in this being reduced to the state where one can not (or no longer) love. Salvation and the victory over death consist in "being again able to love". But this is first of all a relation to Christ. Only when I recognize, lovingly, what *he* has done for me, does my life become again meaningful. Only in the fact that he died in his particular way lies the possibility that at the end, at my death, something has become worthy of God's love, for Christ's sake and yet in me. Thus, my deed, my living and dying, is not primarily related to me but to him. This can be expressed as it is in one of the passages allowed for use in the liturgy of the dead: "None of us lives to himself, and none of us dies to himself. If we live, we live to the Lord, and if we die, we die to the Lord; so then, whether we live or whether we die, we are the Lord's. For to this end Christ died and lived again, that he might be Lord both of the dead and of the living" (Rom. 14, 7–9).

In this sense the spirituality of a Christian death should be far more a devotion to Jesus than is common today. Perhaps we can take here a leaf out of the book of Protestant spirituality. A feature of the theology of martyrdom, expressed on the feast of the first martyr, could be extended and made to apply to all Christian deaths: "He was the first to return to the Savior that death which the Savior deigned to suffer for us." Thus, witnessing to Christ is always the personal confession that anything that may be worthy of love in me is solely due to him. In this sense the life and death of every believer should be prophetic. This spirituality, which in spite of our meager soteriology has remained so very christo-centric throughout tradition, should be the more acceptable today since it implies basically a powerful expression of trinitarian christology. It comes out most clearly in the parallel that occurs so frequently in St John: as Christ stands to the Father, so we stand to Christ. Our death, too, does not take place before an unspecified, impersonal God. Christ's death to the Father, which is the one and only saving deed, makes it possible for us to live and die in personal love and union with Christ, and thus, again through a personal relationship, to be taken up by the Son to the Father. It is this final eschatological situation which shows us that salvation-history cannot be understood as a matter of structures and laws but only as a personal encounter with the triune God.

This leaves perhaps room for the hypothesis that allows for a final and all-decisive gesture on the part of man at death. One would not rightly understand death as it appears in revelation, if one saw it as a final gesture with which man disposes of himself in his own right and under his own control. Yet, in view of Christ's death, this last moment remains open to God's mercy. As the "decisive moment" it can already influence life and lead, without man being able to account for it, to the decisive acceptance of Jesus' death as the only way to salvation. But even if this stage has not been reached in life, that final moment remains an "open" moment. Even there where man has not been prepared for it, at least in appearance, Jesus' death has kept this moment open.

(c) Since Christ has embraced in his death the whole situation of human life and death, it is also possible for him who has no explicit faith in Christ to achieve a positive attitude toward this uniquely redeeming death in his own life and death. I cannot develop this here in detail. When Christ seeks man there where he is in reality, it is understandable that his Spirit will seize the beginning of an as yet inarticulate acceptance of the mystery of God's love in a person still in the grips of a struggle between belief and unbelief, and lead it to an end to which the judgment of God's grace will not deny fulfillment in Christ.[4]

---

[4] The question remains whether in this order of redemption there is not room for a restoration of death in the sense of a creaturely condition

VI

RESURRECTION AND JUDGMENT

Finally, there remains the point of God who is at the same time he who judges and he who fulfills. The correct integration of the position of God as judge in the whole of our eschatology is fraught with difficulties. Not everything that medieval spirituality has brought to the fear of God's judgment is false. It would be a pity if the sounds of the *Dies irae* and the *Libera* lost all their meaning. It is good for me, to know that I am facing a God who is not concerned with my beautiful eyes—who indeed does not "respect the person"—but looks into my heart. I do not know to whom the judgment applies as a threat, but I know that it certainly concerns me. This judgment-piety is not yet false when it pours some fear into man, but only when, in some false and impersonal fashion, it makes God a kind of guarantee for man's pharisaic kind of righteousness, a God who no longer judges man as such but mere factual performances. Yet, without the proclamation of God as judge the eschatological picture is incomplete. For it is precisely this "judge" aspect that makes it possible to integrate too individualistic interpretations of eschatology into the context of salvation-history and to create a meaningful link between death and resurrection.

(a) God's judgment is concerned with the fact that Christ is vindicated. If after Easter there is still room for the day of redemption as day of judgment, this is because every individual human life story must be integrated into the paschal mystery that has already happened in Christ. We already mentioned the cornerstone of this integration when we were talking about the resurrection of the body. God is concerned with man as a whole and as living. Therefore he is concerned also with man's body,

---

that has been restored to its original clarity: the idea of "brother Death", from the Song of the Sun. This would not be death as the final enemy to be destroyed according to 1 Cor. 15, 26, but death insofar as it prevents man's life from becoming a sterile vegetating in a world which will pass according to God's will and may be compared with the falling off of a ripe fruit.

and consequently with what makes this body meaningful: the historical existence of man in a "bodily" world. From the point of view of the judge within whose competence final fulfillment lies, this is a matter of integration. But integration is only possible within the mystery of Christ. Man's eternal existence can only build up in him.

In the past, eschatology has given little thought to this process of bodily resurrection and put it down to a single moment (of course not out of sheer thoughtlessness but with reference to such texts as 1 Corinthians 15, 52). Over against this simplistic view, more recent opinion that resurrection is not a matter of molecules and atoms, present in the body at the moment of death, but that the soul builds its body again out of "appropriate" matter, has opened the way to a more thoughtful exploration of the meaning of this process. What is "sown" is not atoms for the risen body but it is the bodily condition, which has become the shape of man in the historical world, that is entrusted to the earth. On the other hand, it is rightly emphasized that after death there remains no such thing as a soul totally detached from the world and indifferent to the bodily condition. (In some vague way even Scholasticism steered already in this direction.) Karl Rahner speaks of a relationship of the soul to the whole cosmos.[5]

When we take these two points together, does this not mean that the resurrection already begins with the end of the earthly mode of existence? Should resurrection in its temporal sense be placed in the one final moment or is it wiser to see this final great *moment* of Christ as the fulfillment and revelation of the integration of all in the mystery of Christ? Is this integration, which even for those already dead has a "history", namely, the history of the integration of the world to which they belong, not part of the integration into the paschal mystery? The personal history of man is indeed decided at death—whether he belongs to Christ or not. But how his own "shape" in the coming and enduring world will be integrated can only become clear when seen from the angle of the fulfillment of all in Christ. With what

[5] Cf. *Zur Theologie des Todes* (Quaest. disp. 2, Freiburg, 1958), p. 20.

he is, he would already partake in this final "time" in an active way that is decisive for others. But for the full integration of himself he would still need the full complement of his brothers. This would naturally imply a falling off of his activity. In Christ this activity is already pure and complete, and, by derivation, also in those that are assumed into heaven with body and soul. It is not really necessary to stress that all this does not rarify and dissolve the bodily condition of the resurrection. But if the "how" of resurrection can only be understood in the reality of God's Spirit, this means: if this can only be believed in love in the present condition of pilgrims, it becomes necessary to place it in the sphere of *love,* therefore of the Spirit, where alone it can have meaning, and this is the "spiritual" paschal mystery of Christ.

(b) Is it not possible in this perspective to see that here two lines of thought meet which are both brought out by thinking about salvation-history though starting from different concepts, and both reflected in Scripture, namely, the apocalyptic view and the evolutionary view? God remains in his divine mystery the integrator of this history and so the one who fulfills it but the integration grows *within* history. The one line shows the history of how the Father gives to the world the Son of his love, and this reaches its climax in the resurrection of his Son. The other line shows the history of the Son, who, living as man in the world, returns to the Father. Eschatology is the attempt to discover our final place in these two historical processes, a place which is finally made possible and effectuated by the Spirit.

Jordi Pinell Pons, O.S.B./*Barcelona, Spain*

The Theology of Life and Death in the Mozarabic Rite

For the Christian, the final and supreme act of worship on this earth is his death. In many of the chants of her funeral rites, the Church prays to the Lord in the name of the dead man. This is a common feature of all liturgies but especially of the ancient Mozarabic rite. The prayer of the Christian in the moment of his death and the prayer of the Church in her solicitude for the eternal destiny of all her children, these alternate and mingle in such a way as to form one single act: the Christian passing over into eternity continues praying within the Church, and the Church makes her own that ultimate attitude of submission to the plan of God, which is to be consummated in the immortal soul when it is stripped of its body.

In respect of that body, the liturgy, which expresses transcendent realities by means of visible signs, does not merely take account of it but rather surrounds it with tenderness and turns it into an object of veneration. In the lifeless body, the Church sees, above all, the memorial of a life. She does not avert her eyes from the humiliating corruption through which it must pass. But she finds her own reasons to explain the necessity of that disintegration of the body; by passing through it the body will be renewed and reborn into a new life.

That is why the numerous and profound texts of the Mozara-

25

bic funeral rite contain a theology of death indissolubly bound up with the theology of life. On the other hand, it would have been impossible to arrive at a doctrine of death so optimistic and simultaneously so well-founded on motives of faith and hope if the liturgy itself did not regularly, insistently and lucidly present a conception of the next life that made it possible to formulate that doctrine.

I

SPECIAL CHARACTER OF THE MOZARABIC RITE

On this point the Mozarabic liturgy does indeed deserve special attention above all other rites. Prayer and contemplation are constantly focused, above all in the Office, on themes of eschatology; and these are developed with a wealth alike of images and of direct and precise theological statement which must have had a powerful, formative influence on the concept of death held by all those taking part in that liturgy. It must be borne in mind that it was normal for the people to take part in the Divine Office.

A study of this kind is debarred, by reason of its brevity, from giving a complete synthesis of the doctrine of death, found in the Mozarabic funeral rite. On the other hand, the essential materials for such a synthesis are to be found in an excellent work recently published.[1] This article by J. Llopis is of a technical precision that allows the elements of the synthesis to be developed and ordered in various ways as desired. His presentation of the theme, starting from the use made of Holy Scripture in the Mozarabic funeral rites, leaves on one side any doctrinal assertion less directly derived from the sacred books. It does, however, lay down one incontrovertible principle by which the course of all subsequent studies into the content of the texts must be

[1] J. Llopis, *La Sagrada Escritura fuente de inspiración de la liturgia de difuntos del antiguo rito hispánico*, Misc. Férotin (Consejo Sup. de Investigaciones Científicas, Inst. E. Flórez), Madrid-Barcelona, Hispania Sacra, 1966, pp. 349–91. cf. also J. Llopis, "Influencia del salterio en la oración litúrgica. Testimonio de la liturgia funeraria del antiguo rito hispánico" in *Phase* 3 (1963), pp. 201–5.

guided: that the liturgy of the dead in the Mozarabic rite derives its entire theology of death from Holy Scripture.

For this reason, I think that it would be best here to approach the matter from a different direction. We cannot leave the liturgy of the dead simply as a consolation for those remaining behind in this world, or as an encouragement to them to pray with confidence for the dead person. Neither is it enough for it to serve the living as a remote preparation for death when in reality the funeral rites are immediately directed at the Christian who has reached the end of his temporal life.

That demand for authenticity, which must guide liturgical reform in our time, compels us not only to revise what is said of death by the liturgy of the dead, but also to ask ourselves what it is that the liturgy gives to a Christian throughout the whole course of his life that qualifies him, at the moment of his passing over into eternity, to turn to God with that attitude of serenity which the funeral rites presuppose, or ought to presuppose. A revision on these lines ought to make itself felt in the selection and composition of texts and also in the laying down of certain homiletic principles that are necessary if the liturgy is to be fully effective.

II

THEOLOGY IN THE SELECTION OF TEXTS

At least insofar as concerns the selection and composition of texts we find in the ancient Mozarabic liturgy a magnificent example. It serves to show once again how a genuine pastoral sense must be rooted in a theological vision of the Christian that is both profound and coherent. And conversely it makes clear just how far the liturgy goes in forming the Christian consciousness, not merely because it teaches but also because, by giving a focus to the prayer of man discovering himself as an object of the redemption, it necessarily tends to inform his whole life with awareness of its penetration by the mystery of Christ. The largest and most original collection of the Mozarabic texts containing an eschatological teaching, in close connection with the liturgy of praise, is to be found in a series of psalm collects which in my opinion can be attributed to St. Leander of Seville.[2] These prayers were preserved in the ordinary ferial Office and were said principally in morning prayer. They followed the singing of the corresponding psalms and their antiphons. There is no doubt that at the time of their composition they were intended also for Sundays and feast days of the liturgical year, but given the simplicity of the Spanish calendar, these texts, even after their reduction to the ferial Office, would have been very often heard by the faithful.

In them, eternal life is described in terms of the concepts of repose, tranquillity, peace and liberty, pointing out the contrast with their opposites as experienced in this life. But the dominant ideas used in describing the life of heaven are those of gladness and joy. If on the one hand, as has been said, repose and peace, liberty and happiness are presented as the opposites of earthly sufferings, it is, on the other hand, clearly taught that the blessings of eternity are neither more nor less than a prolongation and fulfillment of that joy in the Lord that can be won even in this present life. Possession of, and joy in, God are conditional on knowledge of the truth of God, namely, on faith, which enlightens the soul and leads it, in deep poverty of spirit, to humility. From this there follow the desire and hope of remaining always in the Church, as living members of the body of Christ,

[2] This precious collection, scattered among various Mozarabic sources, comprises more than two hundred prayers of very distinctive content and formal style. We hope shortly to publish our arguments in favor of this attribution to St. Leander. For the sources of the Mozarabic liturgy in general, cf. J. Pinell, "Los textos de la antigua liturgia hispánica. Fuentes para su estudio", in Estudios sobre la liturgia mozárabe (Publicaciones del Inst. Provincial de Investigaciones y Estudios Toledanos, Toledo, 1965), pp. 109–64; J. M. Mora, Bibliografía general. Ediciones de textos, trabajos y repertorios, ibid., op. cit., pp. 165–87. An historical outline of the Mozarabic rite: J. Pinell, "Mozarabische Liturgie", in Liturgisch Woordenboeck, (Nijmegen, 6, 1966), pp. 1796–825. For a more recent bibliography and a study of both history and doctrine, cf. J. Pinell, De liturgiis occidentalibus, cum speciali tractatione de liturgia hispanica (Pontificium Institutum Liturgicum Anselmianum pro manuscripto, 2 vol. Rome, 1967).

and of accepting and loving the grace which is at work in Christians giving glory to God, specifically in the liturgy of praise but also in the observance of justice, in fraternal charity, in zeal for the good of one's neighbor.

Examples

As one among so many examples, let us consider the following text:

> Victor and Lord, O Jesus Christ, whose power extends from sea to sea, grant us to remain in the unity of Your kingdom and, drawn by the sweetness of Your holy teaching, to attain the goal of our faith; and so master our flesh by the bonds of Your law that You may keep safe our mind by justice and peace; therefore, may that peace which came upon the mountains reconcile to You the humble, and may that justice which the hills deserved to see intercede without end for Your suppliants; and thus in zeal for holiness may both these virtues increase among all nations, justice teaching men piety and peace binding them together in the bonds of love, so that justice may keep us safe in this world and peace unite us to Christ in his everlasting kingdom.[3]

Almost invariably, as in the example just quoted, the eschatological theme only appears in the last clause of the prayer. But it is prepared for by a whole series of reflections and petitions and comes at the end to crown every other desire and hope. We

[3] "Dominator Domine Iesu Christe, qui dominaris a mari usque ad mare: concede nobis in tuae dominationis unitate consistere, et doctrinae sanctae dulcedine cursum fidei nostrae perficere; ac sic carnem nostram legalibus frenis adstringas, ut mentem nostram justitiae et pacis ope defendas; pax igitur, quam susceperunt montes, ipsa tibi reconciliet humiles; et justitia, quam videre meruerunt colles, jugiter exoret pro supplicibus; ac sic utraque virtus zelo sanctitatis in populis vigeat, ut justitia informet ad pietatem, et pax vinculis caritatis innectat; ut justitia defendat in saeculo, et pax coniungat Christo in regno perpetuo." Quoted in J. P. Gilson, *The Mozarabic Psalter*, (H. Bradshaw Soc. 30, London, 1905), p. 51; text revised in J. Pinell, *Collectae Psalmorum*, (Pontificium Institutum Liturgicum Anselmianum, pro manuscripto, Rome, 1966), n. 244.

would have to multiply examples to show the variety and wealth of these brief suggestions of the eschatological theme. We shall see subsequently that there is no lack of texts in which it is amply developed, even to the point of becoming the principal object of the prayer. But limiting ourselves for the moment to those other prayers in which it is simply suggested, we must observe that what would most have impressed on the mind of Christians the idea of the serenity of death, was the insistence with which it was shown that eternal life is a liberation from, and compensation for, the sufferings of this world and simultaneously the fullness of that same spiritual joy which can be ours in time.

Let us now consider another prayer, the whole of which deals with the theme of eternity:

The portion of our inheritance, Lord God, consists in Your eternity; and so we beg You, Lord, to keep safe Your inheritance in Your unfailing lovingkindness; give it always as a saving remedy the chalice of that passion You did drink for its sake, that Your harvest of the redeemed may be great as the gifts of redemption are glorious; that we who have been redeemed by Your cross may be forever Your inheritance that You may not abandon our souls in hell but raise them, freed from corruption, to live with You forever.[4]

This series of prayers had in many ways a great influence on the whole Mozarabic euchology, especially on that of the office. It is not therefore surprising that a very considerable number of prayers and blessings in the festal office should also end with

---

[4] "Pars hereditatis nostrae, Domine Deus, in tua consistit aeternitate; unde precamur te, Domine, pietate solita hereditatem tuam conserva; et calicem passionis, quem potasti pro ea, semper ei pro remedio praesta; ut sicut redemptionis praeclara sunt munera, ita redemptorum sit adquisitio copiosa; quique redempti sumus cruce tua, simus perpetim hereditas tua; ut nec in inferno animam nostram relinquas, sed incorruptam tecum semper victuram adtollas." Quoted in F. de Lorenzana, *Breviarium Gothicum secundum regulam beatissimi Isidori*, Matriti, 1776, reproduced in *P.L.* 86, 275; text revised in J. Pinell, *Collectae Psalmorum, op. cit.*, n. 43.

the eschatological theme. We take almost at random a prayer of paschaltide which ends as follows:

". . . so that coming at length to the things You have promised, we who now with sure faith believe in Your resurrection, may deserve to see You our Lord hereafter in the everlasting splendor of Your glory." [5]

In the second Vespers of Christmas, the prayer which begins:

"We have seen Your Glory O Lord, Your Glory as of the only-begotten Son of the Father",

ends as follows:

"Grant to us therefore to be partakers in Your kingdom, to whom You have in this world already shown mercy; and to those whom in Your loving kindness You did visit as redeemer, show Yourself in the age to come a re-warder." [6]

One of the principal prayers on the feast of the Epiphany ends with these words:

"Kindle us, we beseech You, with the saving flame of Your Love so that we, who have even now known You by the gift of Your Light, on fire with the heat of Your love, may deserve to cleave to You forever." [7]

---

[5] ". . . qualiter ad tua venientes promissate, dominum nostrum, quem nunc resurrexisse certa credimus fide, post in aeterna te videre mereamur gloriae maiestate." Quoted in J. Vives—J. Claveras, *Oracional Visigótico*, (Monumenta Hispaniae Sacra 1, Barcelona, 1946), n. 904.

[6] "Vidimus gloriam tuam, Domine, gloriam quasi unigeniti a patre . . . largire igitur, tuo fieri participes regno, quibus es propitiatus in mundo; quibusque pius advenisti redemptor, exsiste in futuro munerator." *Ibid.*, *op. cit.*, n. 314.

[7] ". . . accende nos etiam, precamur, salutifero tui amoris ardore; ut qui te iam dono tuae inluminationis agnovimus, tuae quoque dilectionis

All the ascetic striving of Lent toward its final end is expressed in the following:

"So that, freeing us from the bonds of evil habit You may bring us in the future to the company of all the saints there to be crowned with them." [8]

And the whole expectation of Advent is shown issuing into the same hope:

"And therefore in humility let us await You with longing so that when You come You may take us to Yourself forever." [9]

The same ideas reappear in the texts of the Mass throughout the whole liturgical year.

In the Mozarabic funeral rites there is insistent prayer for the purification of the dead man's soul; it is admitted that he has been weak and sinful. The Church, presenting him before the supreme Judge, recalls, above all, other things that God has done for him: creation, redemption, the gift of faith, the promises of eternity, the sacraments. On the part of the Christian, the Church reminds the Lord of the faith and hope with which he accepted the gifts of God.

"Let him rejoice to have received that which in this life he confidently believed in." [10]

---

ardore flagrantes, tibi adhaerere in perpetuum mereamur." *Ibid. op. cit.,* n. 416.

[8] ". . . quatenus, dum nos malae consuetudinis ligamine reddideris absolutos, sanctorum catervis in futuro consocies laureandos." *Ibid., op. cit.,* n. 568.

[9] ". . . et ideo expectemus te desiderio humiles, ut cum veneris, efficias nos tibi sine fine consortes." *Ibid., op. cit.,* n. 67.

[10] "Gaudeat se percepisse quod in hac vita fideliter credidit." M. Ferotin, *Le Liber Ordinum,* (Monumenta Ecclesiae Liturgica 5, Paris, 1904), p. 134.

The dead body is spoken of with crude realism:

"It is a fearful thing, O Lord, that to You who are the Lord our God, prayer should be made for man by man, for mortal by mortal, for dust by dust." [11]

But the Church does not ask for the salvation of the soul without recalling the necessary restoration and glorification of that same body;

"So that with the coming of that great day of recognition and reward when You will restore all men to life, he may then be found in the company of Your holy patriarchs, prophets and martyrs, crowned with heavenly splendor and that You, having restored his body, may glorify him in Your light." [12]

As we have already indicated, many of the chants speak in the name of the dead man himself. In them are found occasionally sentences of a dramatic character taken from Job. But even more numerous are outpourings of confidence and desire of God:

"Behold I have entered on the way of all flesh so that I must sleep with my fathers and I shall be no more. Remember me, O Lord, from Your kingdom." [13]

"Free my soul from prison, O Lord, that I may give praise

[11] "Temeritatis quidem est, Domine, ut homo hominem, mortalis mortalem, cinis cinerem tibi Domino Deo nostro audeat commendare." *Ibid., op. cit.,* p. 125.

[12] ". . . ut cum dies ille magnus agnitionis ac remunerationis advenerit, quando resuscitaturus es omnes, ibi inveniatur cum sanctis tuis patriarchis, et prophetis, ac martyribus tuis gloria caelesti coronatus, corporeque reddito, facias eum in lumine decoratum." *Ibid., op. cit.,* p. 134.

[13] "Ecce ego viam universae carnis ingressus sum, ut dormiam cum patribus meis, et amplius iam non ero. Memento mei, Domine, de regno tuo." *Ibid., op. cit.,* p. 110.

to Your name. The just await me till You give me my reward." [14]

"I believe that my redeemer will raise me to life and in my flesh I shall look upon my Lord." [15]

"If I go up into heaven, O Lord, You are there, and if I go down into hell, You are by me. Stretch out Your hand, O Lord; free me from the depths of hell." [16]

"Do not depart from me, O Lord my God; do not abandon me." [17]

In her chants, the Church turns also to the dead man, calls him "earth" but invites him to hear the voice of the Lord who will raise him to life:

"Earth, O earth, hearken to the voice of the Lord. May the angels of God take you up." [18]

"May the Lord open to you the gate of paradise so that you may return to that country where there is no death and sweet joy has no ending." [19]

Among the penitential supplications that accompany the bearing of the body to the cemetery, the prayers of the indulgence

[14] "Educ, Domine, de carcere animam meam, ad confitendum nomini tuo; me expectant justi, donec retribuas mihi." *Ibid., op. cit.*, p. 117.

[15] "Credo quia Redemptor meus resuscitabit me, et in carne mea videbo Dominum meum." *Ibid., op. cit.*, p. 121.

[16] "Si ascendero in caelum, Domine, tu ibi es, et si descendero in infernum, ades. Mitte manum tuam, Domine; libera me ex inferno inferiori." *Ibid., op. cit.*, p. 122.

[17] "Ne elonges a me, Domine Deus meus, ne discedas a me." *Ibid., op. cit.*, p. 126.

[18] "Terra, terra, audi verbum Domini. Suscipiant te angeli Dei." *Ibid., op. cit.*, p. 125.

[19] "Aperiat tibi Dominus paradisi ianuam, ut ad illam patriam revertaris ubi mors non est, ubi dulce gaudium perseverat." *Ibid., op. cit.*, p. 123.

stand out. These recall the prayers of the pardon which form one of the most moving parts of the liturgical action of Good Friday. In this way the death of the Christian is shown, ritually too, as related to the death of Christ.

It is thus that, taken as a whole, the Mozarabic funeral rites present a concept of Christian death as a crowning of the sacramental life:

"Living in this world he was signed with the seal of the Trinity";[20]

a death which is simply a transition from the Church on earth to the Church in heaven:

"Just as here by faith he entered into the multitude of Your faithful, so there by Your mercy may he be gathered up into the choirs of angels." [21]

[20] ". . . qui dum hic adviveret signatus est signaculo Trinitatis." *Ibid., op. cit.,* p. 400.

[21] ". . . ut sicut hic eum vera fides iunxit fidelibus turmis, ita eum illuc tua miseratio consociet angelicis choris." *Ibid., op. cit.,* p. 401.

William F. Macomber, S.J./*Rome, Italy*

The Funeral Liturgy of the Chaldean Rite

The Chaldean rite is distinguished among the other rites of Christendom by its archaism. This is particularly true of its funeral liturgy, and this not merely with regard to the structure of the ceremonies, but also with regard to the theology of death and resurrection expressed in its hymns, and, indeed, the fundamental insight into the Christian view of death that gives sense and unity to the whole. Consequently, a serious study of this liturgy has value even for those concerned with the renewal of other funeral liturgies, for they are enabled through it, despite the strangeness of its idiom, to attain, as it were, the very wellspring of their own liturgy which they hope to renew.

The funeral liturgy that this article will be concerned with is primarily that intended for laymen. In all Oriental rites, indeed, the rites celebrated for clergy and religious differ considerably from those for laymen. Some of the differences will, however, be noted as the occasion may demand.

The rites considered will likewise be those indicated in manuscript rituals and the printed text of the Orthodox.[1] There is, indeed, a remarkable uniformity in the manuscript tradition

[1] *Ktaba d-kurrasta d-'annide bnay 'alma*, Trichur, 1954. Parts of the rite for priests have been translated into English by G. P. Badger, *The Nestorians and Their Rituals*, II (London 1852), pp. 282–321.

from the oldest of the 12th century to those of the 19th, and this tradition is faithfully expressed, with but minor variations, in the recent edition of the Orthodox. Even in the latest Catholic edition[2] the changes are scarcely greater. Actual practice, however, especially with Catholics, introduces very substantial modifications, which are themselves of considerable interest from the point of view of liturgical renewal since they illustrate the problems involved in adapting the ancient liturgical framework to the conditions of modern life.

In its traditional structure the Chaldean funeral liturgy consists of four parts, the ritual washing of the body, a vigil office of prayer in the house of the deceased, a solemn procession accompanied by chants from the house to the cemetery, and the actual burial. This structure is derived from very ancient times. The washing of the dead before burial is already mentioned in the New Testament at the death of Tabitha;[3] the vigil of prayer is reported by St. Gregory of Nyssa at the funeral of his sister, St. Macrina, in the 4th century;[4] the funeral procession was a pagan usage Christianized by the Church that is also mentioned by St. Gregory, as well as by other 4th-century authors;[5] and the burial of the dead was a usage taken over by the Church from the Jews.

I

THE RITUAL WASHING OF THE BODY

The modern ritual of the Orthodox still gives highly detailed instructions for the washing of the body of the deceased. These in themselves have no importance except to show the traditional reverence with which the bodies of Christians should be treated. Much more significant is the prescription that follows: "And they clothe him in white garments as on the day of his wed-

[2] *Taksa d-ʿannide ak ʿyada d-ʿetta qaddišta d-Suryaye Madnhaye d-hennon Kaldaye* (Mosul, 1907).

[3] Acts 9, 36–7.

[4] *P.G.* XLVI, 992–993.

[5] *Cf.* M. Righetti, *Manuale di storia liturgica*, II (Milan, 1946), pp. 340–3.

ding." [6] This directive sets the tone of the entire Chaldean funeral liturgy. For a Christian, death is the passage from this world of suffering and sin to the true life of sinlessness and incorruptibility in the resurrection. Hence, as the 9th-century anonymous commentator of the Chaldean liturgy notes, Christians are carried to the tomb, not with grief and lamentations as in the case of pagans who have no hope, but with songs of joy as if to a banquet. [7]

II

THE VIGIL OFFICE OF PRAYER

The vigil office consists of three *cathismata* (roughly the equivalent of Latin nocturns) of psalmody and hymns, plus readings from Scripture. To be noted is the popular character of this office. The psalmody of each *cathisma,* in particular, consists of only two appropriate sections of psalms with a single, brief, invariable antiphon: "O Quickener of the dead, glory to thy name!" The hymns are of two kinds: one is a meditative chant that expresses in a series of rhythmic strophes, each introduced by a suitable psalm versicle, the theology of death and resurrection; the other is a more popular form of lamentation, two or three stanzas sung slowly and mournfully by a cantor with a refrain for the chorus, that frequently expresses the human tragedy of death and gives an outlet to the pent-up grief of the bereaved. Interspersed, moreover, among these psalms and hymns are brief sacerdotal prayers that closely resemble the collects of the Roman rite, except that their theme is almost uniquely the glorification of God, that is, that we may be enabled to glorify him at all times, especially in the face of death.

The scriptural lessons are taken, not from the epistles and gospels as in all other rites, but only from the Old Testament or the Acts of the Apostles. This peculiarity is perhaps due to the fact that the service takes place in the home, for deceased laymen are taken, not to the church, but directly to the cemetery. There

[6] *Ktaba d-kurrasta,* 2.

[7] R. H. Connolly (ed.), *Anonymi auctoris Expositio officiorum Ecclesiae,* II (Corp. Script. Christ. Orient. 76), Romae 1915, pp. 123–5.

are different lessons for men, women and children, most of which
teach the resurrection in one way or another, e.g., Hezekiah's
thanksgiving after his miraculous recovery from mortal illness
and the raising of the dry bones in the prophecy of Ezekiel. The
printed ritual of the Orthodox has an added collection of special
lessons to replace the standard ones in the case of the aged, the
rich, the unmarried, strangers, virgins, and so on, anticipating
the call of the Vatican Council for a wider and more varied
choice of scriptural lessons. The lessons are then followed by
another brief section from the psalms chanted with the same
invariable antiphon as before.

III

DIFFERENT FUNERALS OF LAYMEN AND ECCLESIASTICS

The principal difference between the funerals of laymen and
ecclesiastics lies in the fact that only the latter are brought to
the church. Mass, of course, is celebrated on behalf of deceased
laymen as well as for ecclesiastics, but for laymen this is tradi-
tionally done, not on the day of burial, which is usually the very
day of death, but on the most suitable day that follows, frequently on Sunday. The principal reason, however, why laymen
are not brought to the church before burial is the conception of
the funeral rite as a leave-taking of this world and a journeying
forth to the true life of the future world. Accordingly, the ec-
clesiastic, whose whole life was dedicated to the service of the
Church, is brought to the church to which he was attached and
there takes his leave, and again on coming out of the village in
which he lived. The layman, on the contrary, whose life was
spent in the world, bids farewell to it on going out of his home
or on leaving his village.

IV

THE FUNERAL PROCESSION

The core of the Chaldean funeral liturgy that gives its peculiar
meaning to the whole is the funeral procession, which is a sen-

sible representation of the journey of the Christian from this world to Paradise. In ancient times the deceased was accompanied by the chanting of psalms.[8] The Chaldean Church, however, has substituted a series of eleven processional chants of the type we have already encountered in the vigil office, each of whose strophes is introduced by an apt psalm versicle, giving a meditative air to the whole. These chants are surely very ancient, for they are also found in a Jacobite funeral collection of 823 A.D. and are attributed there to St. Ephrem.[9] Their themes express in various ways the idea that the deceased is not journeying to the corruption of the tomb, but to the glory and joy of the resurrection; this Christ has already effected for us by his resurrection, that is the exemplar and pledge of our own.

Among these processional chants the first and last are focal. The first expresses the deceased's farewell to this world:

"Fare thee well, O temporal dwelling, that cannot save them who possess thee; for I go to see the place of light where the Just who have laboured have their dwelling."

In the funerals of ecclesiastics this is chanted just as the procession leaves the village, whereas with laymen it would more often be chanted on leaving the house. While it and the following chants are being sung, the two choirs that chant the strophes alternately, and the rest who take part in the procession precede the deceased. As soon as they arrive at the cemetery, however, they set the bier on the ground and begin the last chant, which expresses the imminence of the resurrection:

"Our Lord is coming and is raising the dead; and is bringing hope to all the deceased." After three strophes they again pick up the bier and proceed to the grave, but now the deceased himself leads the procession.[10]

The funeral procession, despite the fact that it is the heart of

[8] *Cf.* Righetti, *loc. cit.*

[9] Most of these chants have been edited with a Latin translation by S. E. Assemanus, *Sancti Patris Nostri Ephraem Syri opera omnia,* III (Romae, 1743), pp. 333–59.

[10] *Ktaba d-kurrasta,* 113. The Syrians and Maronites have the same chant at the moment of interment.

the entire rite and gives meaning to the whole, is its most vulnerable part and the one hardest to adapt to the conditions of modern life. This is apparent from other Oriental rites that have reduced the processional chants to a single hymn or have even, as in the Coptic Church, suppressed them altogether. Already in Chaldean manuscripts of the 18th century the practice of anticipating most of the processional chants in the home of the deceased can be observed, but the focal first and last chants, at least, were maintained in their original position and function. Today, with automobile hearses and city traffic, a procession from house to cemetery is no longer possible. The Orthodox still chant the first processional chant as they leave the house of the deceased, having anticipated the others in the house. Catholics in cities, on the contrary, usually transfer the vigil office to the church and simply abandon most of the processional chants altogether. As for the first chant of farewell, they sing three or four strophes on entering the church.[11] At the cemetery, however, a true procession is formed, as far as the circumstances of the place allow, and both Catholics and Orthodox still sing the traditional last chant, "Our Lord is coming . . .", that so well expresses the imminence of the true life of the resurrection toward which the deceased has set forth.

V

AT THE GRAVE

The ceremonies at the grave are dominated by the hope of a glorious resurrection. First, the deacon directs an exhortation to those present to pray for the deceased, that "God, who . . . has taken him in the true faith, may bring him to the goal of all the Just; and when he resuscitates and raises up all who sleep in the dust and allots a good end to all who have been pious and

---

[11] Thus the farewell chant has incongruously been turned into one of entrance. The adaptation, however, may to some extent be justified if the church is considered a type of heaven; by entering the church, accordingly, the deceased symbolically bids farewell to this world.

just, he may call him and set him at his right hand, inscribe him in the Book of Life, include him in the number of the Elect, and join him to the multitudes of them that glorify himself . . ."

Analogous ideas are contained in the collect that follows. A second sacerdotal prayer then prepares for the letting down of the deceased into the grave: "Blessed be the authoritative command of thy majesty that brings to death and restores to life, brings down to Sheol and raises up, and clothes our bodies with glory in the resurrection . . ."

The actual letting down into the grave takes place in the middle of a chanted homily, which is usually a selected portion from the metrical homilies of Narsai, the foremost doctor of the Chaldean Church.[12] They contain scriptural expressions of the hope of the resurrection and vivid descriptions of the Parousia and the separation of the wicked and the just. They have the nature of a meditation at the open grave, and one rather suspects that this reflects a monastic usage.

The officiating priest then takes a bit of earth in his right hand and, addressing the deceased, recites this last blessing: "May God, the Lord of all, who gave the commandment concerning thee, 'Dust thou art, and to dust thou shalt return', himself call thee and set thee at his right hand resplendent in the glory of the resurrection; and may the holy mysteries that thou hast received plead thy cause and win thee pardon at the judgment seat, amen." Concluding the prayer, he casts the earth into the grave, and those that stand about do the same. While they bury the deceased, they sing a final chant that echoes in various ways the hope and prayer for a glorious resurrection. At the end two collects emphasize the same thought, which reappears as well in the final blessing of the grave and bystanders.

Thus the theme of the resurrection penetrates the entire funeral rite. What is primarily considered is the general resurrection of the Last Day toward which the deceased has departed,

---

[12] The three that are found in most rituals have been edited with a German translation by M. Wolff, "Drei Begräbnisgesänge Narsais," in *Oriens Christianus* 12 (1922), pp. 1–29.

but the relation of the glory of that resurrection to Christ's and to his cross is also clearly and repeatedly expressed. By contrast very little attention is given to the condition of the soul between death and resurrection. The particular judgment and purgatory are implied, but in a very indirect manner. The lessons of death, the vanity of this world and the sobering thought of judgment, are not neglected, but they are not allowed to submerge the dominant note of Christian hope and even of joy.

It is unfortunate, however, that the spiritual treasures of the Chaldean funeral liturgy are locked in the Syriac language, which is largely unintelligible to the people. The scriptural lessons, it is true, are already proclaimed in the vernacular, and the prayers present no real problem for eventual translation. But the splendid funeral hymns that contain most of the theology cannot so easily be translated into another idiom that has a different prosodical structure, is associated with different religious chants and expresses to a certain extent a foreign mentality. One hopes, nonetheless, that the Church will not be discouraged by these not inconsiderable difficulties from opening up these treasures to her children in Christ.

Damien Sicard/*Montpellier, France*

The Funeral Mass

The Mass for the dead is a Catholic tradition as widely known during the first centuries as the viaticum and the laying out of the body. But before the 7th century there is no reference to the eucharist which applies explicitly to a Mass celebrated during the funeral or with the body present. The question arises how far, in what form and from what time the funeral ceremonies included the celebration of the Mass. Pastoral care can only profit from the results of such an investigation.

Roman Funeral Customs

Roman liturgical practice in the matter of funeral rites is known to us through the *Ordines Romani,* the books containing the "ordinary" ritual in force in Rome. Until recently only one of these texts was known in the now classic work of Michel Andrieu.[1] But other *ordines* have since been discovered and have been or will be published.

A careful perusal of these texts leads one to the conclusion that Rome did not know of a celebration of the eucharist during the funeral service. The *responsoria missam* mentioned in the

[1] M. Andrieu, *Les Ordines Romani* (Louvain, 1931–61). The text referred to is *Ottobianus latinus* 312, edited under n. XLIX in part IV (1956).

text published by Andrieu,[2] is *responsoria mista* in the *Ordo* of Limoges, *responsoria permixtos* in that of Cologne, *responsoria permixti* in that of Rheinau and all the later rituals. Moreover, if *missam* is not a faulty transcription, one might still ask whether it does not refer to an item of prayer rather than the celebration of the Mass.[3]

On the other hand, what the Penitentials of Theodore of Canterbury tell us about Roman funeral customs may throw some light on the matter. They only mention a Mass on the day of burial in the case of monks and other religious. In the case of laymen, the Mass was celebrated later, on the 3rd day for those that were "good Christians", on the 30th or the 7th— after 7 days of fasting imposed on their relatives—for the "penitents".[4] The evidence of the other Roman *Ordines* gives us the context for the later liturgical tradition. Where the defunct are mentioned we read: "At their Mass, the *Gloria* and *Alleluia* should not be sung." [5] How can we explain this suppression if there were not already a special Mass for the dead?

Where the Roman rubrics are reproduced in a non-Roman environment and add that "the body itself must remain in the Church till Masses have been celebrated for the soul",[6] they insist that one must wait for the Masses to be celebrated, but do not specify whether this refers to a particular Mass, such as a special Mass for the dead would be.

Gallican Funeral Customs

From the 9th century on there are traces of Gallican rubrics

[2] The text says: "Psallant psalmos vel responsoria missam vel lectiones de Job."

[3] Cf. C. Mohrmann, "Missa" in *Vigiliae christianae* XII, 2 (1958), pp. 67–92. Moreover, how can we explain *psallant missam* if we are dealing with a Mass?

[4] Cf. A. Chavasse, *Le Sacramentaire Gélasien* (Paris-Tournai, 1958), pp. 67–70.

[5] Cf. *Ordines Romani* XVI and XVII (Andrieu's class.): "In (Ad) missas eorum Gloria in excelsis Deo nec Alleluia non cantatur."

[6] Cf. the *Ordines* of Cologne, Limoges, Rheinau (9th-10th cent.): "Et ipsum corpus in ecclesia debet esse usque dum pro ipsa anima misse celebrentur."

and one observes that there it was already customary to have a Mass at the funeral.[7] This tradition was taken up by a great number of sacramentaries, of French or German origin between the 9th and the 12th centuries, and during the 13th century it was embodied in the Pontifical of the Roman Curia,[8] and it is from that time on that the usage became universal.

The *Ordines* alone, though, are not enough to find an answer to our question; we should also look at the early sacramentaries to find out whether they contained any formularies specially composed for a funeral Mass.

The First Special Masses for the Dead

So far, the rubrics do not mention a Mass at the funeral or do not tell us what kind of Mass is referred to. What they say may apply just as well or even better to the Mass of the day than to a special funeral Mass. *Ordo XV* (Andrieu), however, contains a notice that seems to refer to a special Mass but without specifying whether the Mass is celebrated actually during the funeral: "For the ritual of the dead, introit antiphon, *Donet vobis dominus requiem sempiternam,* with the psalm *Te decet,* 'Thou hast formed us out of earth', or if there is only one dead, 'Thou hast formed me'. This is the tradition according to the Ordinary or usage of the Holy See of the Church of Rome." [9] The text does not explain whether we have to do here with the funeral itself or simply with a Mass for the dead. The insertion "if there is only one" would seem to indicate a general kind of service for one or more dead. The context, in any case, states on what days funerals and Masses may be celebrated.

[7] Cf. the Sacramentary of St. Denys of Paris (Paris, *B.N.lat.* 2290): "In ecclesia autem requiescet corpus defuncti quoadusque pro eius anima missa cantatur et offeratur ab omnibus quibus fuerit visum."

[8] Text: "In ecclesia corpus defuncti requiescat donec missa cantetur, sed ante missam dicatur vigilia."

[9] "Ad agendas vero mortuorum, antephona ad introitum Donet vobis dominus requiem sempiternam cum psalmo Te decet: ad communionem vero antephona cum ipso psalmo Te decet, De terra formasti nos, si de uno, formasti me. Ista est traditio secundum ordinem vel consuetudinem sanctae sedis romanae ecclesiae."

There are, however, several Roman texts which, without being directly connected with funeral ceremonies, show the existence of special Masses for the dead. First of all, there are the October Masses in the Sacramentary of Verona, called the *Leonianum* (*L*). One particular part of this text (1161) might well have been composed for the funeral of St. Sylvester. The 8th-century Bobbio Missal has a "Mass for a Dead Priest" of which two parts are closely linked with the *Leonianum* while the third one is also found in the Gallican additions to the funeral ritual in the old Gelasian Sacramentary (*V*). This last mentioned text contains 14 Mass formularies (sections XCII to CV, of the third part). Ten of these figures already in the *Leonianum,* at least in Part I, cannot treat of them in detail here. Prof. Chavasse has pointed out the Roman elements in these Masses and the fact that three of them seem to be linked by a single editorship, and date from the 7th century.[10] I merely want to observe that only four of the 68 parts contained in *V* can apply to the day of burial (*diem depositionis*) and that two of these are obviously the result of a clumsy interpolation.[11] None of the Masses contained in *V* can be taken as a special Mass for early Roman funeral rites.

Under the heading "Prayer for a Dead Bishop", the Sacramentary of Hadrian I contains a six-part formulary which was taken over by Alcuin's Supplement and the Sacramentary of Echternach of the 11th century.[12] Only the *Hanc Igitur* of this Mass refers to the day of its celebration as "in commemoration of the departure of the soul of this bishop, thy servant and priest";[13] we have here a commemoration of the funeral itself.

[10] Cf. A. Chavasse, *op. cit.,* pp. 61–71 and 470–95.

[11] They are the two prayers of the formulary CV (Cf. A. Chavasse, *op. cit.,* p. 69). The two other cases occur, one in formulary XCII, 2, the other in the *Hanc igitur* of formulary XCVIII. Both cases might refer to the funeral rather than the day of the funeral.

[12] This Mass is found under n. 224 in Lietzmann's edition.

[13] "Pro commemoratione depositionis animae famuli et sacerdotis tui illius episcopi."

These observations confirm what we have already learned from the *Ordines*. In the beginning there was certainly no special Mass for the funeral service in Rome.

The Formularies Contained in the Gallican Documents

Most Gelasian Sacramentaries of the 8th century, Alcuin's Supplement to the *Hadrianum* (*Alk*) and many other texts of the 10th-11th centuries more or less freely reproduce Masses nn. XCII to CV of the third part of the old Gelasian Sacramentary (*V*), as they are found in either *V* or *Alk*. Two Gelasian Sacramentaries of the 8th century must be singled out because they are the only ones to insert a Mass formulary within their funeral ritual. These are the Sacramentaries of Gellone and of Berlin. The first one (*G*) gives under the heading "Prayers for Mass before the Body Is Buried" four prayers of which the first and the last (headed "Another Prayer after Communion") are but two prayers of the ritual contained in *V*. The only prayer of these four which seems to belong strictly to a funeral Mass, the Secret, "We beg thee, Lord", is in fact the same as that in Mass CVI of *Alk*'s "Mass for the Anniversary of a Dead Person",[14] and is very close to several formularies of *V*. The fifth part, which closely resembles *V, CIV*, 2 (n. 1686 in Möhlberg's edition), and the first prayer in the funeral ritual of the *Hadrianum* deserves to be quoted: "Lend the ear of your goodness, O Lord, to our prayers, and grant the soul of your servant N. . . . remission of all sins that he may rest in your refreshing light until the day of resurrection. Through Jesus Christ", etc.[15] This prayer asks that the defunct be granted rest in God's refreshing light in the expectation of the day of resurrection, and thus it shows a more elaborate eschatology than that common to the prayer

[14] Missa in anniversario unius defuncti. The Secret and *Hanc Igitur* of the Phillipps Ms. of Berlin reproduce the phrase: *"cuius hodie annua dies agitur"* without further specification.

[15] "Inclina domine praecibus nostris aures tuae pietatis et animae famuli tui ill. remissionem tribue omnium peccatorum ut usque ad resurrectionis diem in lucis amoenitate requiescat. Per dominum."

literature of that time. Nevertheless, we can still not be certain that these first Romano-Gallican texts contain a special funeral Mass.

The same holds for some isolated Gallican documents which I must mention here. The Mass for the Dead of St. Denys (*D*) which most scholars attribute to the beginning of the 8th century[16] contains the prayer *Deus cui proprium est,* a Secret and a long Preface that recall those of the Gelasian Sacramentary (Möhlberg's ed., nn. 1610–12). The so-called Pontifical of St. Alban of Mainz (10th century) contains a Secret and two Postcommunions taken from Mass XCIX of *V* (2 and 4) and from the Hadrian funeral ritual (*Annue nobis*). The Missal of Robert of Jumièges (12th century) inserts a Mass in its Gallican Ordinary, of which the three prayers are borrowed from *V*. Mass CV, also of *V,* provides a number of sacramentaries, like those of Amiens, St. Gereon of Cologne (9th-10th cent.), Nevers, Prudentius of Troyes, Tyr, Hamburg (11th cent.) and Jerusalem (12th cent.), with prayers for their Mass on the day of burial which follows their funeral ritual or is incorporated in it.[17] The Pontifical of Paris (13th cent.) and that of Toulouse (14th cent.) use a Mass which has taken over two of the three prayers from the funeral ritual of the Hadrianum.

The "Prayers at Mass" of the Sacramentary of St. Denys of Paris (about 875) borrow only one prayer, the Postcommunion *Prosit Domine quaesumus,* from the collection of Masses for the dead of *V,* without any significant changes. There is no exact parallel in the Roman texts for the other two prayers. They show the importance attributed in non-Roman milieus to the invocation of God's mercy and forgiveness: "We beg you, Lord, have pity on the soul of your servant N. and, having delivered him from our mortal contagion, give him a share in eternal salva-

---

[16] Paris, *B.N.lat.* 256, fol. 103 ᵛ. Edited by Delisle (1884), De Bruyne (1922), Beyssac (1934) and Combaluzier (1955).

[17] The texts referred to a nn. 1, 4 and 6 of Mass CV of the third part of the Gelasian. L. C. Möhlberg, *Liber Sacramentorum Romanae Ecclesiae* (Rome, 1960), nn. 1690, 1693 and 1695.

tion." [18] "Prayer over the oblations. May this offering, Lord, deliver the soul of your servant N. . . . from all the sins and vices of the human condition since, through this sacrifice, the sins of the whole world are taken away." [19]

Most Gallican Sacramentaries from the 9th to the 12th centuries reproduce the "prayers at Mass" of the Sacramentary of St. Denys of Paris or another kind of formulary that appears from the 9th century on in the Pontifical of Aurillac and these link the prayer *Deus cui proprium est,* which already appears in the Gallican Mass of St. Denys, with a Secret and a Postcommunion unknown in the Roman documents.

There is no room here for the prayers which occur in the old manuscripts that contain funeral Masses. Their content is rich. Yet, it would appear useful to conclude this article with the conclusion that the history of the texts shows no convincing evidence for linking the funeral liturgy with a special celebration of the eucharist. Historically speaking, it would seem that it is rather the death itself of the Christian than his funeral that is seen as having a link with the eucharist. The liturgy of the Word of this Mass of the Dead consisted of the reading of the passion of the Lord, thereby evoking the death of the Lord himself. Its prayer was the old Roman prayer at death and recalled the evangelical episodes of Lazarus and the good thief (Luke 16 and 23). This was normally concluded with the viaticum where communion was taken under both kinds.

Could this old Roman prayer of "recommendation" of the dying person not guide our prayer in the future as it did in the past?

"Lord, in whose presence all that dies lives, and for whom our bodies do not perish in dying but are changed for the better,

[18] "Quaesumus domine pro tua pietate miserere animae famuli tui ill. et a contagiis mortalitatis exutam in aeternae salvationis partem restitue. Per."

[19] "Super oblata. Animam famuli tui ill. domine ab omnibus vitiis et peccatis conditionis humanae haec absolvat oblatio, quae totius mundi tulit immolata peccatum. Per."

we beg You to command that the soul of this Your servant be taken up by the hands of the holy angels into the lap of Your friend, the patriarch Abraham, to be raised on the last day of the great judgment; and from whatever he may have contracted against You in this region of death through the ruse of the devil, cleanse him with Your fatherly love and mercy. Through Jesus Christ." [20]

[20] "Deus apud quem omnia morientia vivunt, cui non pereunt moriendo corpora nostra sed mutantur in melius, te supplices deprecamur ut suscipi iubeas animam famuli tui illius per manus sanctorum angelorum deducendam in sinu amici tui patriarchae Abrahae resuscitandam in die novissimo magni iudicii; et quid de regione mortali tibi contrarium contraxit, fallente diabolo, tua pietate ablue indulgendo. Per."

Antonio Savioli/*Faenza, Italy*

The Final Resting Place of Deceased Christians

I

PRELIMINARY REMARKS

In the course of my pastoral ministrations and a few years' professional experience as an architect, I have encountered various types of attitudes toward the mystery of death and have evaluated the interpretation many Christians place on the theme of tomb and cemetery. When I was a young curate almost all the relatives of the deceased members of the parish would turn to me for the epigraph on the memorial card (but I shall not burden the reader with even one of these inscriptions). When I became interested in symphonic choral music, my taste had been accustomed to Gregorian modalities, and it suffered genuine disillusionment on hearing the different Requiems—even those of great renown—on account of their frighteningly mournful counterpoints.

The contrast was further heightened when in my rare rural ministrations—finding sufficient motives to wax ironic on the immoderate funeral dirges of priests—I chanced to enter some rustic cemetery among the piquant fragrance and bright hues of the flowers of the fields, and the rank grass surrounding indigent tombs nestling under the shadow of the church. When obligations of study caused me to frequent some large cities of central and northern Italy—Rome, Florence, Bologna, Milan—I be-

came acquainted with the great cemeteries known as "monu-
mentali", and with the sacraria of churches.

A fine example of the latter is the Florentine church of the
Holy Cross, wherein the ancient tomb integrated with the altar
has in more recent times become a prime example of pagan
rhetoric; while the deceased ancients sleep in the crypts and lie
in pavemented figures of marble or bronze, the "strong" mod-
erns are evoked by cold statues representing them immersed in
their temporal pursuits.[1] The monuments to the popes in St.
Peter's—excluding reasons of exhibitionism—are generally in-
spired by the concept of celebration.[2] In Florence I loved the
little cemetery "Della Misericordia", on the outskirts of Soffiano,
because I finally encountered therein a truly Christian practice
—the "common" Mass. The layout of the cemetery is not such
as to ignore either private graves or interments in sepulchres;
but large chapels with the image of a saint and the altar keep
watch over the corpses, and here on a designated day every
month the living gather together for Mass and Communion.

I would have preferred to omit these vaguely impressionistic
thoughts; but they seemed to merit recording—if for no other
reason than as an introduction to our subject.

II

ANCIENT AND MODERN FUNERAL PRACTICES

After recalling a few elements of ancient and modern funeral
practices I will give an up-to-date bibliography.[3] On the subject
of the tomb we can draw useful pointers from Christian antiquity in Rome. The prince of the apostles was buried in a

[1] This theme provided the inspiration for the poem *Dei Sepolcri* by
Ugo Foscolo, published in 1807.

[2] The recent monument to Pope John XXIII does not escape this characteristic in its very complicated iconographic style.

[3] The best Italian contribution is the text *Arte funeraria* (Milan, 1958),
enriched with a pictorial anthology and a bibliography which demonstrates the paucity of recent works. Among the works in the collection
is cited the book well-known to architects by R. Aloi, *Architettura
funeraria moderna,* in the Hoepli series from Milan.

common necropolis and his tomb became the pole of a con-
stellation of those who sleep in Christ. The same thing happened
in the case of the tombs of a few martyrs. In the catacombs
special treatment was reserved for the tombs of bishops and
popes. Distinctions such as archosolium, sarcophagus, and family crypts in underground cemeteries are explained by adverting
to economic reasons: anyone who had greater economic means
provided a richer tomb for himself.[4]

Some—with poor historical sense—might interpret these distinctions in a classicist key; but in reality, the "cohabitation" of
poor and rich in the ancient Christian cemeteries is indicative
of a charitable custom, the emergence of a community sense
that has perhaps never again occurred in the history of tombs
and cemeteries.

One or two examples are also found in the medieval Christian
tomb. Notwithstanding the custom of distinguishing burials according to hierarchy or merit, it is still possible to find a positive
element not only in the desire of believers to discover the repose
of death in the shadow of churches or in chapel crypts, but in
the community sense expressed by the burials of ecclesial communities and lay fraternities. Witness to this is had in the pave-
ment windows which are still numerous in ancient churches.[5]
The growing social disproportion, the ever more rapid decline
of the community and Christian sense, and the triumph of in-
dividualism signalled the affirmation of the "single" tomb. We
need not dwell upon this sad monologue which not even the
new French civilization on the threshold of the modern era
succeeded in curbing.[6]

[4] A reflection of the ancient custom at Rome, as background to a certain interest for the knowledge of funerary organization, is in Ippolito
concerning the right of the poor to burial and the duty to pay the grave
digger and the price of marble; cf. B. Botte, *La tradition apostolique de
Sainte Hippolyte* (Münster Westfalen, 1963), p. 86.

[5] See the stupendous tomb-glass of the burial of canons of the Cathedral
of Naples (1475) in the Basilica of St. Restituta, illustrated in *Arte
funeraria, op. cit.,* p. 91.

[6] The decree of the French legislature which regulated burials is of
June 12, 1804; the articles of the text on medical regulations which concern cemeteries are numbered 75, 76, 77 of section X, and are published
in the *Giornale Italiano,* n. 276 (October 3, 1806). These items are found

Pagan usages, never abandoned and not even reabsorbed, are still the most evident manifestations of our funerals and tombs today: inconsolable and despairing grief, pictures of the deceased in realistic form, preservation of corpses, monumental tombs. Today we have laudatory panegyrics and poems about the deceased—whether rhetorical, false, or prolix.[7] Even an attentive exegesis of the epigraphic theme (invocations, exclamations, literary citations) would reveal deceptive and negative aspects from the Christian point of view.

III

CONSIDERATIONS CONCERNING THE CEMETERY

Considerations concerning the tomb find their counterparts in the cemetery theme; the accent, however, falls on the city-planning aspects insofar as cemeteries represent one of the most notable spiritual and organizational viewpoints of the urban context. However, most public administrators continue to equate them with a common civil service, basing their policy on purely physical concepts and reducing the content to a problem of hygiene. The populace on their part insist on aspects that were dear to romantic phantasy, legends and fear-inspiring phenomena—as a whole, a custom unworthy of a community of believers and baptized.

G. Bardet (1958) reflects on this theme and discovers therein motives of profound Christian inspiration; however, he is more

---

in the speech by F. Trevisan on *Il Carme dei Sepolcri e altre poesie di Ugo Foscolo* (Milan, 1898), pp. 47–49; cf. the note by G. A. Martinetti on epitaphs.

[7] A curious example is the following epitaph: "Here united with the ashes/ of the parent and brother/ those also would be found of/ A.Z./ in conformity with his fervent wish/ whereas to make it complete/ would not be the work of opposing laws" (communal cemetery Church of Faenza). The style is contorted; the concept documents the unpopularity of French laws in Romagna. A fine example of funerary epitaphs or Christian inspiration is given by C. and G. Costantini in *Fede e Arte*, vol. I (Rome, 1945), pp. 275–90.

discerning in his criticism than in his suggestions.[8] Obviously, a Christian funereal art devoid of falsehood and scandal will not be realized until the faithful exemplify a theologically exact attitude toward death; in the hypothesis that it is possible to find a community of baptized at this level of formation, it is legitimate to set apart for them a spot in the midst of a neo-pagan and pseudo-Catholic cemetery. But how will we express "the overall equality of bodies in the face of death", and the idea that "nothing must seem definitive"? Is the mode of burial really essential to a Catholic expression when there is some way of verifying faith in the future life and in the resurrection of the body?

A study of R. Auzelle takes up a consideration of the rational mode of burial in cemeteries from the city-planning point of view, in harmony with ecclesiastical legislation.[9] The ever more widespread usage of burying the corpses in sepulchres of rock or cement, camouflaged by marble monuments, belongs to a belief far removed from the Christian view since it is based on the idea of semi-conservation. Insofar as this custom prolongs the process of putrefaction it constitutes the principal cause of the continuous extension of cemeteries and their chaotic aspect. If cemetery grounds were not cluttered with "unclean" sepulchres and served for the pure and simple inhumation of cadavers, they could accommodate plants, flowers and gardens; such cemeteries in the midst of inhabited areas would constitute sufficiently vast reserves of greenery, oases of tranquility and meditation. On the city-planning level, cremation would provide the perfect solution to the mode of burial, but it encounters the opposition of the Church in some areas.[9a]

However, in order that real and true burial can be accepted

---

[8] *Arte funeraria, op. cit.,* pp. 7–12.

[9] *Arte funeraria, op. cit.,* pp. 13–20. This resumes the thesis upheld at the Institute on City-Planning at the University of Paris in 1940: *Les problèmes de sépulture en urbanisme.*

[9a] Such opposition varies in degree from country to country. However, since the hierarchy has already authorized cremation in different dioceses and published a rite for cremation, general ecclesiastical approval is clearly indicated. In England, 40,000 Catholics were cremated in 1967.

as a valid function by city planners, it must be generalized and imposed in the interests of the community. As far as the religious problem is concerned, Auzelle affirms that "the Church has for a long time not concerned herself with the cemetery . . . ; the semi-conservation of the burial niche does not seem to pre-occupy her. Nevertheless, she must decide whether she wishes to give interment a different spirituality than the one supposed by cremation".

G. Gresleri[10] also finds modern necropolises solitary and sorrowful, and private sepulchres and mausoleums are elephantine expressions of the sign and symbol of human greatness; the community of repose has given way to the stronghold of the individual, functional bureaucracy and storage technology; nature, greenery and flowers have been replaced by technocratic paradigms such as dimensions, height, number, agency and fees; pedestrian pathways conducive to respite and meditation have become straight roads as in the bleak planning of mechanized cities.

The new cemetery interpretation should evidence and translate the community concept as the stimulus for the vertical dilatation of each person's life on this side of death and on the other. City-planning-wise, the cemetery is an organ which participates in the general economy of the inhabited area, and as such bears a relation to the city or metropolitan area, a relation which is individualized and rediscovered within the context of a natural landscape. If we were to succeed in translating into city-planning and architectural terms the sense of a community of sleepers, we would greatly diminish the danger of lapsing into negative solutions of death, proper to societies of great opulence (American cemetery-parks), or indulgent to the romantic and individualistic version (German cemetery-woods), or, finally, incapable of overcoming the pagan tone of interpretation (Mediterranean cities).

[10] G. Gresleri, "Il cimitero" in *L'edificio sacro per la comunità cristiana* (Brescia, 1966), pp. 174–184.

V. Rovera studies the cemetery in existing canonical laws.[11]
The place that houses the bodies of the faithful must be sacred,
that is, a blessing intrinsically transforms the cemetery (hence
the appellation holy ground), withdrawing it from profane
usages and reserving it in an exclusive way to its proper end.
The intimate nature of such a constitutive blessing is as a sacramental. Furthermore, since the cemetery is sacred, the purpose
of the cult of the dead is equivalent, at least under certain
aspects, to the worship of God. The burial, which is an *officium
humanitatis,* is raised by Christ to an *officium religiosum,* that
is, an act of religion, part of divine worship.

Not only the rite and ceremonies but the very burial itself
pertains to the religious order, and as such demands to be accomplished through a sacred rite and to be concluded in a sacred
place. Burial provides a better expression of the Christian faith
in the resurrection of the body, corresponds with scriptural
events (burial of the body of Jesus), and interprets almost to
the letter a few living and operative ideas of the Judaeo-Christian
tradition, such as those of the body-seed, earth-mother, and
death-repose and sleep.

These relations obviously find justification and development
on the symbolic and not on the realistic level. Generally speaking, there exists no natural or revealed reason that absolutely
excludes cremation. The principal concerns deriving from the
use of burial are of a city-planning nature, following upon the
phenomenon of urbanization and of a hygienic nature on account
of the practical difficulty of establishing cemeteries in locations
which would not damage the underground hydric layer and in
conformity with the direction of dominant atmospheric currents.

"The living are in fear of the dead and, above all, afraid of
death," writes G. De Menasce.[12] This accounts for the clearly

[11] V. Rovera, "Il cimitero nelle prescrizioni canoniche" in *Arte funeraria, op. cit.,* pp. 44–50.

[12] G. De Menasce, "Urbanistica e pensiero cattolico" in *Urbanistica,*
n. 42–43 (February, 1965), p. 144, at the paragraph "Polis e necropoli":
"I am thinking of the cemeteries on the lawn in front of the church, of

separated dualism: city of the living—city of the dead. There are cities in which the dead remain among the living, cities that embrace cemeteries in their boundaries. This peaceful cohabitation, this tranquil and homeopathic presence, full of discretion and sane familiarity, produces truth and allows one to establish oneself in the truth of human destiny. Architects who are not disposed to share the fears and prejudices of city dwellers should seek to decongest those "senseless districts" that constitute the large urban cemeteries, by providing small neighborhood cemeteries where "children could play among the tombs and where mothers could unaffectedly say a requiem or two as they darn their socks".

I will not dwell upon other bibliographical data since they would add nothing new. Besides, literature on city-planning is chary of references, and works such as those of Lavedan and Giedion, merely to cite some examples, ignore the subject, although elements of a judicial nature could be deduced from the ideologico-formal basis they obey.[13]

---

certain English churches; of the small cemetery of Trinity Church hemmed in by the skyscrapers of Wall Street in New York; and I am thinking of the old cathedrals which offered hospitality to the living and the dead and where the dead did not consider it a profanation to be trampled on by the comings and goings of the faithful."

[13] In *Pierre sur pierre* by G. Bardet (Paris, 1945), cf. the cemetery-garden of K. Hippenmeier, at Zurich, married to the topography and divided into sections. The same author in *Problèmes d'urbanisme* (Paris, 1948), p. 62, reproduces the plane geometry of Sabaudia, a city projected and constructed in the Agro Pontino between the two wars; the cemetery still appears outside the urban context. See in *Il cuore della citta* (Ciam, Milan, 1954), on p. 67, the cemetery of the crematorium of Asplund in Stockholm, definite cemetery-heart, even if of a special type, and on p. 109 the cemetery of the farming village of Nagele (Netherlands), traditional from the distributive point of view. As an example of indifference, I remember in number 14 (1954) of *Urbanistica* the two studies on the communities of the Roman countryside and the Laguna Veneta, documented with the best drawings and photographs; the structural analysis of the aggregation makes no allusion to cemeteries.

IV

THE ORIENTATION OF VATICAN II

Let us pinpoint the orientation of Vatican II. The Christian cemetery is a complex reality which is seen under many aspects. This present volume itself demonstrates many facets of the prism. The references to the Council are not limited to the citation of article 8 of the *Constitution on the Sacred Liturgy* but extend to all those passages from which we can extract the Church's thought on this matter in all its renewed freshness. Basically, the word, "cemetery", which is not explicitly mentioned in the conciliar texts, insofar as it is expressive of the material place of temporal convergence and necessary transit for every man, is always to be understood whenever the Council speaks of life and death, sin and redemption, baptism and resurrection.

The Christian people are to be re-inculcated with communal sense, the paschal characteristic of death and the eschatological perspective of the Pilgrim Church.[14] Death, for believers, is a participation in the paschal mystery. Baptism has initiated a movement that will terminate in death, which, after Christ's example is a passage from this world to the Father. Sorrow accompanies death; but the thought of, and union with, the agony of the redeemer fills it with hope in the resurrection.[15] The Christian funeral—hence tomb and cemetery—will have as principal components the joy achieved through faith in the participation of the deceased in the glory of the risen Christ. This gives rise to the sacred character which the Church desires to be conferred on the tomb and on the terrain that receives it and so becomes the place of repose. This doctrinal vision is underlined in the existing liturgical formulas (with a few reservations for the most recent ones) and obviously evidenced to the greatest degree in those that are presently being proposed.[16]

For a comparison between the conciliar ideas and those that

[14] L. Della Torre, *Corso di Liturgia* (Brescia, 1965), pp. 173–81.

[15] *Constitutio liturgica cum commentario* (Roma, 1964), p. 156, commentary by P. Jounel.

[16] Cf. *Paroisse et liturgie*, n. 3 (1966).

can be deduced from today's Code, see the customary sources, which appear more or less interesting as regards the architectural-city-planning for tomb and cemetery. For example, Fattinger is most detailed in explaining the requirements of the Code for the term "cemetery".[17]

Allow me to examine instead an ancient liturgical source; its doctrinal substratum seems to me to be completely well-balanced in the fusion of the proper components of the funeral theme. In the *Pontifical* of William Durand [18] for the solemn blessing of a cemetery, the bishop pauses before the five crosses and pronounces a prayer each time. The brilliant *cursus* does not impede us from collecting the links of the splendid doctrinal context of perfect conciliar ideas, which are hence suitable for proposal for the consideration of architects and city-planners.

The human body and the earth: "You formed the human body from the earth . . . you assumed it . . . you dissolve it on the earth . . . you will resurrect it from the earth . . ." (cross toward the north).

Burial and baptism: ". . . may those who have received the sacrament of baptism . . . have here the seat of repose . . ." (cross toward the south); ". . . may those who through baptism have already been buried together with you . . . rest in peace . . ." (cross toward the north).

Cemetery, place of repose: ". . . the human bodies which will here repose in God . . ." (central cross); ". . . this cemetery in which the bodies of your servants are to repose . . ." (western cross); ". . . those who have entrusted their own body to repose in this cemetery . . ." (cross toward the south).

Final resurrection: ". . . to the bodies of those who . . . await the trumpet of the first archangel . . ." (eastern cross); ". . . after the resurrection of the souls and bodies . . ." (western cross); ". . . so that on the day of the last judgment

[17] R. Fattinger, *Dizionario tecnico-pratico di liturgia* (Rome, 1954).

[18] M. Andrieu, *Le Pontifical romain au Moyen-Age, t. III, Le Pontifical de Guillaume Durand,* Studi e Testi 88 (Vatican City, 1940).

the souls will rise with the bodies . . ." (cross toward the south); ". . . Lord Jesus Christ, who from the earth formed the human body . . . and from the earth will resurrect it . . ." (cross toward the north).

Joys of eternal life: ". . . may the human bodies . . . after the course of their lives merit the joys of eternal life . . ." (central cross); ". . . to the bodies . . . grant perpetual consolation . . ." (eastern cross); ". . . as you granted the promised land to the people of Israel . . . so may the faithful after the resurrection . . . deserve to enjoy eternal happiness" (western cross); ". . . may the souls together with the bodies be reunited with the saints" (cross toward the south).

The very recent Belgian directory for the new ritual for funerals, cited above, does not differ substantially from the *Pontifical* of Durand; the texts indicated for scripture readings can be grouped around the themes of resurrection, the eucharist and life eternal, hope, and sorrow turned into joy. By virtue of the developments in eucharistic doctrine and piety, the eucharist very fittingly assumes a special place in the funeral liturgy. Funeral foods and refreshments were taken in even by the early Christians in honoring the most ancient rites; the remnants of such usages are still among us today.[19] In reality, the deceased partakes of the heavenly banquet in the glory of Christ, represented on earth by the eucharistic banquet. Typical of the Middle Ages was the eschatological component, which explains the presence in Durand of the trumpet of the first archangel and the last judgment, though fused within a context of hope and salvation. This is one theme I would not neglect were I in the process of composing funeral liturgical texts.

We might observe that both Durand and the Belgian directory are rich in suggestions for pictorial artists. Here are a few examples from the ancient *Pontifical,* prayer at the cross toward the north:

[19] In the zone of Faenza, an area in Ravenna, on November 2 a little sweet is confected in the form of a walnut, called "al favett di murt" (the bean of the dead), and eaten by all as a ritual.

Lord Jesus Christ, who from the earth formed the human body	creation of Adam
assumed it through the redemption	incarnation, passion, and death of our Lord Jesus Christ
and will resurrect it from the earth	final resurrection
deign to consecrate this place as a participation in your burial	Jesus is placed in the sepulchre

From the Belgian directory: the eucharist and eternal life.

canet enim tuba et mortui resurgent incorrupti	final resurrection
cum Christus apparuerit . . . tunc et vos apparebitis . . . in gloria	the elect
omne quod dedit mihi Pater non perdam ex eo	the good shepherd
Ego sum panis vivus qui de coelo descendi	institution of the eucharist

It is a question of making intelligent use of this marvelous theme, transfiguring its letter, shaping its moments into cycles, taking away its motives without losing the clarity of things signified.[20] In substance, the value to be discovered and to be restored to the tomb is that sacredness which is non-generic and not in an immanentistic key, and which coming from the Christian doctrine on death offers itself to men as an experience of faith and the light of hope.[21]

[20] Under this aspect, the most learned modern interpreter known to me is Adolfo Wildt; see the marbles of the tombs of Tibiletti and Cornex in the Cimiterio Monumentale of Milan in *Arte funeraria, op. cit.*, p. 77.

[21] P. R. Régamey, *Art sacrée au XXe siècle?* (Paris, 1952), p. 417; a

I believe that the fact of community—the transparent foundation of the life of believers—is to be sought by considering the location of cemeteries in respect to urban overcrowding; in other words, the city-planning solution to the problem of cemeteries is not indifferent to the degree of a society's communitarian maturity. It does not appear to me indispensable to establish *a priori* a certain mode of burial, nor to have recourse to the hypothesis of the neighborhood cemetery. Instead, it is indispensable to take account of the practical tendency on the part of the population to spread out all over the territory, a tendency which seems to me to favor solutions in harmony with the faith of the believers.

The neo-technological age is committed to decentralization as regards both industrial and residential locales. This process will grow in intensity in the future, causing an entirely new society to evolve toward a final adjustment. The large cities will be transformed into tertiary centers, with motorization favoring the formation of residential centers in the suburbs within a certain radius around urban centers. The city-region will be the place for diverse specializations, rendered homogeneous by the existence of socio-economic factors.[22] A study of these forecasts leads to the thought of a type of city-planning which conceives the city for communal man while it respects the single man, not as an assemblage of initial little cells for an ideal man without neighbors but one whole organism wherein the infinite parts each collaborate with each other.

The principles of method and the formal models that must govern the phases of the organic development will be generally variable; but there are questions for which the choice of method is dictated without alternative. For example, zoning according

---

note refers to the November 1949 issue of the review *Art sacrée,* dedicated to cemeteries and tombs.

[22] J. F. Gravier, "Accentramento e decentramento" in *Relazioni del seminario "La nuova dimensione della città regione,"* Stresa 19–21 gennaio 1962, ILSES (Milan, 1962). See also by the same author *L'Aménagement du territoire* (Paris, 1964).

to function—following Nairn[23]—will be abandoned in favor of zoning according to character, which permits the founding of small urban buildings differentiated by every elementary unity with the possibility of being gathered into ever more ample formations until the principal buildings are formed. According to this organic process of growth, the principal buildings in turn are aggregated in formal configurations which permit the establishment of a well-founded relation between city and suburbs, between inhabited areas and natural surroundings.

Cemeteries should be provided in the most suitable corners of the region, on levels of elementary unity, wherein the relation of inhabited areas to uninhabited areas is integrally transformed. This statement of the problem might seem harsh; but I believe it is a way that offers concrete possibilities to the idea of De Menasce, replete with human content, and of Auzelle-Bardet insofar as the technical aspects of the problem are concerned. In this way the block of megalithic necropolises is broken, cemeteries for the new urban communities are realized and structured like gardens, private furnishing is simplified, and the sacred character desired by the Church is conferred on them. The ritual consecration could also assume forms differing from the traditional ones, but the cross always retains its highest expressive meaning, insofar as it renders visible that paschal mystery on which man's salvation depends.

[23] I. Nairn, "Problemi della trasformazione della città in regione" in *Relazione del seminario . . . , op. cit.*

✠ Theodor Filthaut/*Münster, W. Germany*

Proclaiming the Resurrection in Our Cemeteries

I f anyone needs to be convinced that present-day Christendom gives little thought to hope in the resurrection, he has only to go looking for visible signs of this belief in our cemeteries. There, if anywhere, we should find tangible evidence of Christian belief in the resurrection of the dead. When we realize that in apostolic times the resurrection was the core of the gospel message (cf. 1 Cor. 15, 1–58), we have every right to expect that believers would display this belief with special intensity at the graves of their deceased.

The Distressing Evidence

What, in fact, do we find in "Christian" cemeteries and at "Christian" graves? We find that signs of the resurrection are few and far between, whether we are dealing with Protestant or Catholic sites. Nor is this a new phenomenon, restricted to our age.[1]

If we set aside the non-religious symbols in our cemeteries— images of the deceased, statuary, etc.—then the predominant token of faith is the cross. Catholics also like pictures of the

---

[1] Cf. Rudolf Pfister, *Die Friedhof-Fibel* (Munich[2] 1954); Otto Valentien—Josef Wiedemann, *Der Friedhof: Gestaltung, Bauten, Grabmale.* (Munich 1963); Erwin Panofsky, *Grabplastik: Vier Vorlesungen über ihren Bedeutungswandel von Alt-Agypten bis Bernini* (Cologne 1964), pp. 43–106; since 1956, the periodical *Friefhof und Denkmal* (Kassel).

saints, of the Blessed Virgin in particular. But doesn't this wide-spread preference for the cross contradict our previous assertion? Isn't the cross a symbol of Christian faith and Christian hope, especially if we consider the essential connection between Jesus' death and resurrection as described in the Bible? It certainly is, but unfortunately these considerations play little part in our cemeteries.

For the most part, cemetery crosses are not symbols of hope in the resurrection. Quite often their use is purely for the sake of convention or decoration. The change that has begun to take place in recent years is not much in evidence. To an overwhelming extent the cross is a symbol of sadness, suffering and death. This does not exclude the possibility that it may also be a token of resignation and consolation, testifying to the believer's faith in God's merciful love. To this extent it bears witness to the note of hope in our faith, but it would be a mistake to equate this type of hope with hope in the resurrection of the body.

What it really represents is hope in the continuing life of the soul before God "in heaven". Numerous inscriptions at grave-sites wish "eternal life" or "eternal rest" to the deceased. The feast day of November 2 is commonly known as "All Souls Day", and no one takes this amiss. "Save your soul" seems to be the dominant message of our cemeteries. According to this outlook, only the soul is important and decisive.

Now this particular brand of Christian faith in salvation is one-sided, narrow and misleading in several important respects. The effect of this dualistic outlook, which exalts the soul and scorns the body, is deep-rooted and ominous. An aura of melancholy and resignation pervades our cemeteries, and the well-tended grounds cannot change that.

Just think for a moment. Cemeteries are the resting places of dead bodies; but nothing is said there about these "earthly remains", these "fleshly garments", from which the souls have departed. Our cemeteries give the impression that Christianity, like many other religions, is a religion of the spirit, a religion that regards matter and the body as things beneath man's dignity or unimportant. Hence, the feeling of impotence or futility that is conveyed by our cemeteries. How could it be otherwise, since the faith embodied in our cemeteries seems to overlook the salvation of the whole man and the salvation of the whole world?

Our cemeteries reveal the gap between the gospel message and the religious outlook of many Christians today. Faith is a joyous, confident, triumphant expectation that a fully renovated world is on its way. Why do we not find this spirit more often in our cemeteries? Graveyards, of course, are not the place for unrestrained merriment. But shouldn't we find there some measure of the joy that Christ bequeathed to his disciples (Jn. 15, 11)?

Belief in Bodily Resurrection

Here we cannot delve into the causes for this diminished awareness in the resurrection of the body, even though such an inquiry would be a real eye-opener for theologians, preachers and teachers. But there can be no doubt that it is a fact, and that it pervades many circles of Christian piety. More than one public-opinion poll on contemporary piety has shown that the vast majority of those who profess adherence to some Church do believe in some kind of life after death—however vague this belief may be. But a majority of those polled felt they could not believe in bodily resurrection.

In these instances we are not dealing with people who have only slight contact with their Churches. A surprisingly high percentage of them are regular Churchgoers. The polls would indicate that the situation in our cemeteries reflects popular belief; the faithful are uncertain about bodily resurrection or have, at best, a vague theoretical belief in it.

Additional evidence lends strong support to this contention. They are small things, to be sure, but their significance is often overlooked entirely. Consider the whole set of customs connected with the burial service. Consider the religious pictures and memorial cards that are found in people's homes. Note the predominance of the cross and of Marian motifs. Where do we find any hint of the resurrection? Where do we find reference to

Christ's resurrection and his second coming as indications of the general resurrection or the creation of a new earth?

All this is truly disturbing. Theology, preaching, catechesis and even the liturgy have failed to express a central tenet of faith. Or perhaps they, too, are plagued by the same defects and omissions? In recent years many theological treatments of the resurrection and its significance have appeared. But this does not necessarily mean that popular preaching and catechesis have picked up these ideas and given them due attention. Any study of recent German books containing popular Easter sermons would soon disabuse us of any optimism on this point.[2] Moreover, the fact that the funeral service was not resurrection-oriented motivated the recent Council to demand its revision.

Necessary Reforms

How can we introduce the hope-filled belief of resurrection into our cemeteries? To answer this question, we must first tackle the underlying causes of the present problem. We must find out why a note of fatality pervades our cemeteries.

To begin with, those who preach and proclaim the Word must reflect on the biblical message of the new creation in Christ. They must bring their own belief and preaching into line with this message. If there is no reform in preaching—in liturgical gatherings especially—there can be no renewal of popular belief in the resurrection, and hence no renewal in the funeral liturgy. The important thing here is that the resurrection message be preached all year round, not just on Easter, and that it be given a prominent place in the funeral liturgy. This message must also be integrated into the contemporary setting. Due consideration must be given to the problems and objections posed by men of today with regard to this doctrine.

Then we must tackle the cemeteries themselves.[3] When all the

[2] Cf. F. Kamphaus, *Von der Exegese zur Predigt: Die Bedeutung der neuen Evangelienforschung für die Predigt, dargestellt an den Oster-, Wunder- und Kindheitsgeschichten* (Mainz 1968).

[3] Cf. Werner Lindner, *Der Dorffriedhof: Wege zu seiner Gesundung* (Kassel 1953).

members of the Church truly accept and live the doctrine of resurrection, a reform of our cemeteries will necessarily follow. As with most things, a start must be made somewhere; indeed, a few initiatives are already under way. Here I shall mention a few practical possibilities.

If a church or chapel adjoins a cemetery, its whole configuration and outlook should proclaim the resurrection and eternal life. It must express hope primarily, not sorrow and sympathy. Statues, emblems and scriptural texts can perform this function; and the same holds true for the tombstones. At the very least, a Christian cemetery should bear witness to the spirit of Easter; it should not be simply a graveyard.

We might also mention the large cross that is located in the center of many cemeteries. The cross is not just a symbol of death. It is also a symbol of new life and of victory; it is the wood from which the world obtains salvation and joy (Good Friday Liturgy). This is what the cross signifies, insofar as it is a symbol of Christ's passion and death. Whether this full symbolism can be expressed in the artistic form of the cross is another question. In any case, there is no doubt that the entrance to the cemetery can set the proper tone. Over the entrance to one cemetery, for example, we read the words of Christ: "I am the resurrection and the life."

As for the monuments themselves, here the faithful have their chance to bear witness to their hope and faith. Before we go into concrete details, however, I should like to briefly discuss what "resurrection" means in our present context. Hopefully, this explanation will satisfy one possible objection to our insistence on the resurrection motif: that it would lead to monotonous repetition in our funeral art.

This objection might well be valid if "resurrection" referred solely to the event that took place long ago in Jerusalem: Jesus' return from the dead. However, neither the Bible message nor the liturgy's representation of it is restricted to this isolated historical event. Instead, "resurrection" means the process which began with Jesus' resurrection, which has gone on unceasingly since then in those who believe in him, and which will eventually culminate in a wholly new creation at the second coming of Christ. It is the new, imperishable, restored world that God is creating through Christ, in the power of his Spirit.

This restoration of the world is a "resurrection"; in other words, it takes place through a process of destruction and death. The new lays hold of the old and transforms it; and the ultimate result is "a new heaven and a new earth" (Acts 3, 21). This all-encompassing panorama clearly indicates the essential connection between grave and resurrection. If we are to really understand salvation-history as a whole, we cannot overlook its material aspect, as we pointed out earlier.

Because this aspect is critically important, and because men apparently tend to overlook or reject it (consider Paul's experience in Athens, Acts 17, 32, and the whole history of Christian piety), we must stress it all the more and distinguish it from the notion of the soul's afterlife.

We find a paradoxical situation. The statements of Sacred Scripture stress the resurrection of the body and its ultimate culmination in the arrival of God's kingdom. In modern-day Christianity, however, the resurrection of the dead and the restoration of the world mean almost nothing; but much attention is focused on the life of the soul after death (purgatory, heaven, hell, beatific vision, etc.). The uncertainty and anxiety of the contemporary Christian outlook—vis-à-vis the world, science, education and culture, sexuality, etc.—are rooted in its *de facto* disavowal of the resurrection of the body. If the eternal life of the soul is the goal of existence, then there is no real basis for a positive attitude toward the world and its various spheres.

Many aspects are worthy of serious attention insofar as the artistic side of the question is concerned. Here we might well single out one important motif: giving honor to God. Christian hope and faith are not concerned solely with the salvation of mankind and the salvation of the world. However important these themes may be, they are not the only ones involved nor even the most important ones. Like every aspect of faith, the

Christian's hopes for the future are centered primarily on God. They are meant to give praise and honor to him, for resurrection and restoration are his work.

Salvation is only the human side of a process which, from God's viewpoint, involves the revelation and victorious arrival of his kingdom (cf. 1 Cor. 15, 24–28). Full salvation entails that "God may be all in all" (1 Cor. 15, 28). Thus, to preach the resurrection properly is to bear witness to the power and love of God, "who created heaven and earth" and will re-create them once again.

This broader understanding of the resurrection provides the motifs for artistic composition, and they are many. To restrict art work to the details of Jesus' own resurrection (the empty tomb, the angel, the sorrowing women, etc.) would be to misconstrue and impoverish the resurrection message. It would also be a mistake to aim solely for narrative art focused on a particular datum of history. The aim is not to faithfully depict some historical event, but to proclaim and expound the salvific meaning of Christian hope.

How can this be done? We can use graphic and non-graphic art, abstract and pictorial art. We can use appropriate inscriptions on the tombstones, as well as symbols and portraits. To depict the intangible aspects of the resurrection, we can use appropriate words from Scripture (e.g., Jn. 11, 25; 1 Cor. 15, 42–44; Apoc. 21, 5), from the liturgy (e.g., the Easter liturgy), from hymns and from poetry.[4] These texts are not meant to be purely decorative or to fill up empty space; nor do they require accompanying symbols and illustrations. They often proclaim the message more plainly than the latter do. Well-chosen and well-executed inscriptions can be fine esthetic contributions to funereal art.

The invisible world of faith can only be glimpsed through

---

[4] An anthology of such resurrection texts is presented in this author's book, *Zeichen der Auferstehung: Zur Erneuerung der christlichen Grabmalkunst* (Mainz 1965), pp. 36–41. There one can also find examples and bases for resurrection symbols and pictures, on pp. 42–49.

signs and symbols. Symbols, then, are particularly appropriate for the proclamation of the resurrection. A few such symbols are the cross, the laurel crown, the lamb, the hand of God and the sun.

Insofar as portraits are concerned, they, too, are only symbolic witness to the resurrection. Besides graphic pictures of Jesus' resurrection, we might also portray Old and New Testament figures, e.g., Jonas, Lazarus and the young man of Naim.

The artistic quality of the tombstone is also an important question, but we cannot go into it here. Let us just note that it is important for both esthetic and religious reasons. The new world that is on its way will be one of spotless beauty, and we must keep this in mind when we try to bear witness to it. Today many of our cemeteries sharply contradict this point.

Some object that good-quality headstones would involve considerable expense, but the argument is not convincing. There is no reason why we have to provide lavish artistic productions, and there is no reason why the stonecutting industry should sell tasteless or insipid products. Standardization is not necessarily inimical to beautiful and meaningful end products. Beauty of form and meaningfulness should be sought at every grave site.

Ladislaus Boros, S.J. / *Zurich, Switzerland*

Some Thoughts on the Four Last Things

Our rethinking of the burial liturgy should not limit itself exclusively to its theological aspects. We should also take account of the spirit of contemporary Christian piety. The following meditations are printed here as an example of the type of thinking we believe any new burial liturgy should make room for. Boros introduces the meditations themselves by making five initial comments. Their purpose is to suggest the manner in which the contemporary Christian should approach all questions concerning the end of time.—THE EDITORS.

I

1. *The End Is but the Beginning*

The key message of the new covenant is that in Christ a wholly new dimension of existence has opened up. We call it heaven. Heaven is something that grows and matures in the children of God, the friends of Jesus Christ. Now that Christ has come, mankind is no longer susceptible of explanation in terms of the apparent facts of his earthly existence. His life is created for heaven, for a condition that is close by and yet— or rather for that very reason—still beyond his reach. Everything that precedes heaven—all the seeking and groping of which the history of mankind and of each individual being is largely constituted—is simply birth. The world itself is formed only when man enters heaven. We do not yet live, in the truest sense of that word; we cannot yet see or hear or fathom life's real content; true life is not ours yet, but it is on its way toward us. The essence of humanity and the world is still ahead.

75

2. *The World Is Set for Perfection*

The world is still undergoing the pains of birth. Out of an original unit of existence the cosmos is developing toward life. And life perfects itself by transforming itself within man into spirit. The spirit becomes itself in that it acknowledges God and pledges itself to him in love. In the union of man the cosmos is snatched into the eternity of perfection and completion, a condition in which God is visible in all things. The universe is a unity of created being, and creation has not yet ended. God creates the world by endowing it, in the course of a continuous development lasting millions of years, with the power to lift itself toward him. Human history, and the process of development in which the world becomes itself, are salvation-history: the slow birth from the earth's womb of that which is eternally valid, the content of eternity. There is no respect in which the evolution of the cosmos can be called profane.

3. *Creation Is a Process Based on a Christological Foundation*

In answer to the question: "Why did God become man?" the Creed replies: "For us men and for our salvation he came down from heaven." We see that two reasons are offered: first, "for us men", so that man can be more fully himself. And then: "for our salvation", so that he might deliver us from sin. These are the two primary functions of Christ in salvation-history.

Subsidiary to these two primary functions the Creed lists others. God became man so as to lead our human existence to perfection. Sin or no sin, the incarnation would have taken place. But as mankind has burdened itself with sin, which is to say, because man made himself remote from God, God had to atone for our sins before he could perfect what we are. It was therefore necessary for him to become our redeemer. This second, retrospective, historically conditioned salvific function (the redemption) does not make his eternally foreseen and decided life act (perfection and completion) redundant, unnecessary: Christ remains he through whom our species is brought to total maturity.

The journey to perfection has been in process since Christ's death.

Christ raises mankind, and thus the cosmos that expresses itself through us, to the realm of perfection. Christ is the summit of created being and that toward which the world's every movement tends. He draws the world's energies toward himself, urging them forward and ever closer to perfection. In this sense, too, Christ is *Deus elevans*. Referring to this cosmic Christ, the Letter to the Colossians says: "In him all things were created, in heaven and on earth [the cosmos] . . . all things were created in him and for him . . . and in him all things hold together." Inexorably and in all respects the cosmos moves toward Christ. Christ is the predestined world. The movement of being narrows down over the aeons, becomes ever more compact and concentrated as it approaches the one pivotal point, the omega point, the Word become flesh.

The time that precedes his second coming is a period of preparation for the formation of man. The total ongoing development that converges in the historical Christ embraces the length and breadth of the cosmos and of history, and thus all reality. The Christ–orientated cosmos wins life and achieves the perfection of its being as man (the world becoming man); mankind is gradually evolving to a state of greater awareness, to a greater facility for decision-taking, and therefore is ever more conclusively confronted with its God (man becoming man); in the incarnation the God-Man united in himself the world's and mankind's total forward-looking thrust and conducted it, through his exodus, death, resurrection and ascension, to the final perfection (God becoming man). This then is the basic structure underlying the creation of a Christ–orientated world.

4. *Perfection as a Limitless Advance*

Utimate perfection (heaven) is participation in God. But no created being is capable of exhausting what God has to offer. There will always be a distance between created being and God.

Thus, even in heaven, apparent satiety is also a new beginning, the onset of a further search, the herald of a yet greater fulfillment to come. In essence, therefore, we should conceive of heaven as an unbounded dynamic in which fulfillment so enriches us and so extends the soul's thirst and awareness, that it is at once capable of yet greater fulfillment. The search for God is eternal, and God remains eternally something greater than we could ever become or apprehend. A God discovered is no God. On earth we seek God in order to find him. In heaven we seek him having found him. To prompt us to seek and find him, he is hidden. To urge us to seek him having found him, he is immeasurable. Eternity is therefore a continuous search for God. In heaven, all that was static becomes uninhibited and eternally perpetuated forward motion. There is no torpidity in heaven, for perfection is eternal transformation, a condition of endless, uninterrupted dynamism.

5. *Christian Eschatology Is a Message of Joy*

With Christ's resurrection, the future fate of the world is determined. Our path lies inexorably heavenward, no matter whether we are conscious or anonymous Christians—in other words, whether our existence is consciously or unconsciously a life in Christ. Transient though the world's works are, the ultimately enduring is at work. Our gropings always pay off. "Nothing can separate us from the love of Christ," that is to say, nothing but the rejection of that love. Such are the dimensions of the resurrection's gift and promise. "I have opened a door," Christ tells us, "that from now on no one can ever again close." However weak the flame of sincere love, it illuminates the heavens. No hope shall be disappointed, and nothing lost to us that in our lifetime we voluntarily gave up. In a world such as this, our world, there is no reason for despair or timorousness. The whole meaning of Christianity could be expressed in this definition: it is the faith through which God perpetually affirms mankind's fundamental longing, indeed surpasses it to such a degree that our most ambitious hopes and dreams seem as nothing.

In this somewhat telegraphic manner I have tried to suggest how a Christian might consider the events that characterize the end of time. The Christian should shake all lurking fears from his mind, for in entertaining them he is entirely misdirecting his attention. Similarly, all questions connected with the "teaching on the four last things" should be approached in the spirit I have tried to suggest under the above five headings.

II

1. *Purgatory as the Breakthrough to Clarity*

Death is the moment in which all those existential irrelevancies that a man collects during his lifetime are sloughed off so that he is faced with himself as he really is, with that in himself that is eternally durable. His successes, power and riches crumble into dust. Suddenly he finds himself without any external props. He becomes aware of his innermost self, as though of the blood pulsing through his veins, its pulse throbbing in his ears. Dazed, and as though gripped by fever, he can still make out the world he once knew, though with exhaustion seizing every sinew; an almost suffocating dizziness and lassitude blurs its faces and forms into shadowy visions. Boundless weariness presses harder upon him and indiscernible shapes now billow around him. He no longer has the energy to break out of his loneliness; his limbs are weighed down with the invisible shackles of a nightmare. His loneliness is total, more extreme than anything he ever knew in his lifetime. Around him the known and loved faces are powerless observers of the pitiless vortex of loneliness that grips him ever tighter as he enters the remotest outposts of time and space.

Such is a man's death. No longer can he cry for help. He is as bewildered now as a small child locked into a darkened room, shut off from outside help and unable to help itself. He can see no way out of the grey mists of immeasurable spaces into which he has fallen. The measure of his sense of isolation is such that he has even become a stranger to himself. The laboriously achieved fruits of a lifetime are no longer his to conjure with, and the roles he once played are now played out. His total being is given over to the minimum that still stirs within it: his longing, his need for help and his situation as one in the hands of absolute mercy.

Earth has neither creature nor agent capable of mediating or detracting from this encounter between man and his true self, and man himself is now unable to erect those old defenses with which he used to protect himself from himself and, in so doing, himself from God.

What then is left once a man has surrendered himself utterly? The answer is suddenly clear: man is left with what he had surrendered—his selflessness. This, the basic inspiration of his life, now comes into its own: all his moments of disinterested behavior reassemble to form a continuity of selflessness that now becomes his true self. The times in which he stood by a friend in need, and all other occasions when he offered himself out of love; the experience of no longer belonging to himself, the bewildering moments and periods of misery and loneliness, the readiness to weep with the distressed and rejoice with the happy, in a word, the sharing in the humanity of others—this now is all that remains to him.

We call this state purgatory. It is the process of ultimate submission that every lover knows. Purgatory is man's encounter with his true self, the consolidation of total existence into essence, the instantaneous passage to total selfhood that is the essence of death, the anthropological and existential aspect of the death process. But because a man cannot be so utterly "himself" without at the same time experiencing, in his own process of becoming truly man, the reality of the incarnation, his self-encounter develops through Christ into an encounter with God. This is not an additional aspect of the death process but rather the revelation of the integration of the human reality with the being of Christ that comes about through grace. Through encountering himself in total honesty, which means himself divested of all existential irrelevancies, man meets Christ.

2. *The Judgment*

The discovery of the Christ-dimension of our existence will be quite as astonishing as Matthew suggests (25, 37ff.), when he reports how the righteous (but also the unrighteous) ask: "Lord, when did we see thee hungry and feed thee . . .", naked, sick, in prison, and so on. It will seem to us then as though the most momentous deeds of our lives were done unwittingly.

Were we to take Christ's words at full value, we could expand this situation, Christ's own conception of the judgment, into a fully-fledged theology of the encounter with Christ which takes place in the hidden or unnoticed moments and events of our lives. The judgment will lay bare that dimension of our deeds which flows directly into Christ, transcending the transient nature of their actual performance. The ultimate level of our experience, of our hopes and wants, of our demand for friendship, kindness, involvement with others, and particularly of all selfless actions, is Jesus Christ himself.

A fresh theological presentation of the nature of Christ's presence in us should be the chief task of contemporary theology. But I shall limit myself here to the mention of one particular and frequently forgotten item in the proclamation of faith—Christ's "descent into hell". The notion indicates at once that Christ's entry into our world is total. He descended even to that point at which the deepest roots of reality unite. "Descent" is meant here in an existential and metaphysical sense—we should think of some point that represents the fundament of all created being, of all natural forces, of all historical and personal relationships. It was the ultimate move in Christ's willed experience of time and space, of immersion in mankind's nature and world of reference, and in these respects the logical extension of his incarnation. There was no heaven before Christ died. Access to God was blocked, as the Letter to the Hebrews observes. Christ's death razed the barriers and God returned to his own, penetrating all things, so that even those recognized him who so far had lived only at the world's pleasure, prisoners of his absence.

In death man shakes off the immediate limitations of human nature, bursts out of his three-dimensional world, perceives wider relationships, enters a plane on which the original fire of creation burns, where all relationships start and end, where the heart of the universe throbs. Through penetrating to the depths of the world, Christ entered among all those who had lived before him. And they knew him immediately. At once the light that recognition, freedom and decision bring, flooded out the darkness: millions of years of time, the thunderous sigh of creation, achieved its aim. The world was no longer as before. Christ pervaded it. He is the mysterious center of all growth. From now onward, every death and every grain that dies in his death is a mergence with Christ. And every selfless act, every helping hand, every surrender of self in deference to something bigger, is faith, redemption and partnership in Christ.

By becoming the world's basis, Christ created a new and redemptive situation. The encounter with him occurs in all human situations, and in them, too, the redeemed world emerges: heaven. It is from this point that we should work out the whole ecclesiology, a complete theology of the sacraments (milestones of the encounter with Christ), of piety within our world, of our encounter with one another.

The judgment is the revelation of the essence of things, of the true orientation of the human heart, and therefore is the encounter with the ultimate ground, with Jesus Christ.

That is putting it in abstract language. Let us try to understand it more closely. Suddenly we become fully aware of that in us which endures, and in this we see that all our impulses were movements of God's heart within us. In death, therefore, we plunge into something we had always known, a "familiar" world we had experienced often, around which our dreams had circled, a world of ultimate truth we had always supposed lay behind the collection of things, events and people that had constituted our total experience. All such knowledge is present in death as we found it within our actual experiences: every smile from one we loved that when it happened suggested a degree of joy we knew we could never contain; every movement of affection that a parent ever knew, that love and friendship ever expressed; every longing that a thing of beauty ever awakened; the distinctive passions of the seasons as they modulate through summer and winter, spring and autumn, the thunder of the mountains, the valley mists, the tempers of the sea, the wonders of profligate nature—the forces that roused us in all these experiences we become aware of in death in one fantastic radiant beat of knowledge. We recognize at once that here we are at home—always were. That unity of knowledge and love that now echos those movements of our soul was always the inspiration of our dreams and longings: it was never anything else but Christ.

Nothing else counts now. Everything else has dropped away, no longer impedes us, can do nothing to trip us as we enter enduring happiness. That is the judgment. How simple things are at bottom! Judgment amounts to no more than the message of joy.

With this somewhat tangled train of thought behind us, we can now move on to a consideration of hell.

3. *Hell*

Hell is not something that God awards us retrospectively as a punishment for our sins. It is not some horrifying combination of vertigo, fire and asphyxiation. It is simply man himself; man, that is, who equates himself with what he is, with what he can do of himself, experience within himself. Hell is the mode of existence of a man who seeks happiness within himself. But it is this extended into eternity. For eternity he neither possesses nor wants for anything but himself. For the living, hell is not the threat of something awful existing outside us but simply a projection of our own pettiness. And he who every day experiences his own pettiness must remind himself that he might be heading for hell. It is possible for me to drown in my own self, to identify myself with my own nothingness. If I do that, I shall be lost.

God is too great to damn anyone. There is no reward for rejection—and reward it would be if God were to take our pride seriously. Hell is not a place but the heart's disposition. Everything lives in heaven because it is for heaven that God created the world. But heaven is experienced with the sensitivities of the dominant personal disposition all of us fashion for ourselves. The poor man will discover his magnificence, and the man who kept his riches will have to live with them.

You can't "go" to hell—only to heaven. He who can endure heaven—who knows how to receive much and give more—is in heaven, lives in the joy that the ability to love creates, the happiness of living for others, the bliss that does not feed on possessions. Heaven cannot be endured by those who lack the courage to love.

4. *Man—the World's Center*

Man can achieve salvation through love for God. In doing this he surrenders himself to that which his love affirms—not his transience, but that in him which is beautiful, worthy of affirmation, valid: the "heart". Man's "heart" is the mystery of his existence, more basic, more profound, more inclusive than anything purely spiritual: spiritual it may ultimately be but it never shakes off the profound depths of its own unique life experience. In the enduring love of God, man ("resurrected" man) is the union and summit of all nature, the highest expression of all cosmic relationships, of the world's total meaning. Nowhere is love's eternal point of reference so meaningfully and radically implied as in the Christian doctrine of the last things. Who can grasp the immeasurable significance of Paul's statement that the Spirit is "poured into our hearts"; or that the body (not the spirit) is a "temple of the Holy Spirit"?

Christ's resurrection heralded the beginning of the last days. To be true to our calling, which is to love God, we must live now as though we were already in heaven. We must live, therefore, as friends of Christ. Christ himself spoke of this ceaselessly. Our mission and destiny is to live a life of love.

Jesus, God become man, called the life he promised us by various names—the kingdom of heaven, the land of the living, perfect peace, the fulfillment of our wishes, ceaseless mercy, being with God. Our way there is through liberation from self, meekness, mercy, integrity, peacemaking, hungering and thirsting for justice. These are the basic qualities of love, and through them man becomes himself by giving himself. That was all Christ taught.

Luis Maldonado/*Madrid, Spain*

Further Liturgical Reform

Thanks to the latest Instructions from the Roman Curia and to the reports from the *coetus* set up by the *Consilium*, we can now foresee the conclusion of a first stage of liturgical reform. This stage will have been characterized by two fundamental tasks, the translation of texts and the simplification of rites.

As always happens in any collective historical action, before some people have even started moving, others have already reached the goal and are launching new movements to take them far beyond it. We have here a primal datum, the evolutionary datum, of which people are steadily becoming more and more conscious, to the point of finally accepting it as inescapable. It entails a practical conclusion that is already unmistakably clear in the field of ecclesiology: reform is not an occasional event but rather a permanent state.

What will be the characteristics of the new stage that will follow on the present one? It is not all that difficult to give an answer to this question. Recent times do show us this: that reform develops according to a peculiar dialectic that consists in transforming what existed merely *de facto* into something *de jure*. The result is that one always has two strata coexisting, one on top of the other: the present, already beginning to be dated, but having the authenticity of an unassailable legal status, and the future, already inaugurated but still destitute of any kind of juridical cover, perhaps also with its true metal debased by impurities that time has to refine away. It is the analysis and comparison of these two strata that helps us to discern the line of evolution.

The word, the liturgical text, has to take precedence over rite, over gesture. This latter will achieve an elemental simplicity, an evangelical transparency and starkness.

The great problem, therefore, is that of the texts. To have the texts in translation presupposes an extraordinary advance. But once in their "ideal" nakedness, they cannot hide how extremely vulnerable they are. In plain words, they are the expression of particular epochs of Christian faith, venerable indeed but remote from, and alien to, our present evolutionary situation as believers. The ancient tradition of the *lex orandi lex credendi* applies here inexorably, and the effect is erosion. The formularies of the liturgy are the expression in prayer of a given faith, spirituality and theology. Our faith, our spirituality and our theology today are on new and very different levels.

Within a formulary one can, even if a little artificially, distinguish three layers, as it were: the words, the ideas, the structure. By translating we have changed the words. A new stage is at hand in which the ideas will be changed and modified. The structure will remain, (e.g., that of anaphora, litany and so on). Then comes a period, eminently creative, of composition of texts. In such a period, it is of prime importance to have one's ears open to the Spirit moving in the Church, the Spirit who enlightens the faith of the Church so as to give a genuinely authentic expression in prayer to the consciousness of faith.

Some of the great acquisitions of present-day theology and of the history of the contemporary Church ought to have a liturgical "precipitate": the theology of the world, of the secular, of history, of the event, the new and deepened understanding of grace, of the supernatural, of Christology, that is to say, of Christ as *Kyrios* of all reality.

All these great theological acquisitions run together and lead in one direction which, as far as concerns the liturgy, can be expressed in the following formula: the classical distinction between the profane and the sacred has to be rethought at the deepest level. It is worth dwelling on this point. Here is the key to the new climate that is coming in. The sacred has always been taken to mean that which is set apart for and by the divine presence, set apart from that which has no such presence, that is, from the profane. But contemporary theological studies, especially those of Karl Rahner, on the supernatural [1] have shown us with a quite new power that, since Christ, this presence has, as it were, overflowed over the whole of reality, breaking down every barrier that could have held it captive, kept it within bounds, and that it has in consequence ceased to be the exclusive property of the sacred or, more precisely, of the sacred domain. In this sense one can even say that Christianity desacralizes. Thanks to the incarnation, the human condition has become the material and the concrete site of God's historical self-manifestation. Thanks to Christ, all of human history is enclosed within the love of God; it is caught up into the absolute and gratuitous presence of the divine mystery, this presence being one radically distinct from that derived from creation in the strict sense; the latter form of presence would be natural, the former is supernatural.

This presence in a certain sense sanctifies the profane and the temporal. This does not mean that it ceases to be profane reality and becomes something sacred. There is a *tertium quid*, namely, the profane made holy or introduced into a sanctifying "medium".

This presence of grace in the depths of each man, believer or unbeliever, which Rahner has termed the supernatural existential and the transcendental, as opposed to the categorical, consciousness, grounds the existence of an anonymous, or, as Schillebeeckx puts it, an implicit Christianity[2] throughout the sphere

---

[1] K. Rahner, "Natur u. Gnade," in *Orientierung* 14 (1950), pp. 141–45; *Natur u. Gnade* (Schriften z. Th. IV, 1960), pp. 209–37.
[2] K. Rahner, *Die Anonymen Christen* (Schriften z. Th. VI, 1965), pp.

of the profane. The concrete human world, considered as an
area distinct from the Church, is, for all the ambiguity of its
position and in the midst of its rootedness in sin, the objective
expression, not sacral but nonetheless holy, of mankind's communion with the living God. The Church, for her part, is the
expression both direct and sacral of that same reality. The relation between the Church and the world, continues Schillebeeckx,
is not to be understood as a dialogue between the religious and
the profane, between the supernatural and the natural, the "of
this world". What is given us is rather a dialogue between two
authentically Christian and complementary expressions of one
same and single theologal life that is hidden in the mystery of
Christ, namely, the ecclesial expression and the worldly expression of that single grace. Rahner makes this further point: the
world is deprived of the numinous but not of sanctity.[3] The
sacral or sacred goes on existing in the sacraments, in Scripture,
in the Church. But this sacral reality is simply the existence in,
as it were, a state of reflexive consciousness, of the sanctification
or divinization of the profane world that has been freely and
graciously established by God.

Similarly Congar confessed in the last edition of his *Jalons
pour une théologie du Laicat* (Paris 1964, p. 652) that, were
he to take up again today the question of the relations between
creation and the kingdom of God, he would have to criticize
the categories of the sacred and the profane. The reason, he
adds, is the fact that for the Christian there is nothing profane
(pp. 666–8).

One can also see how Père Chenu has opted for the category
of the holy as the one that best expresses the peculiar character
of middle term between profane and sacred, which creation,
the world and history have now acquired in Christ and because

---

545–55; K. Riesenhuber, "Der Anonyme Christ nach K. Rahner," in
Zeitschr. f. kath. Theol. 84 (1964), pp. 286–303; E. Schillebeeckx,
"L'Eglise et le Monde," in *DO-C 142* (1964).

[3] K. Rahner, *Der Mensch von heute und die Religiones* (Schriften
z. Theol. VI, 1965), pp. 13–14.

of Christ.[4] Other authors who give the impression of having taken up distinct positions really differ simply in terminology.[5] Finally let us remember, to take a not far distant case, how Père de Chardin was one of the first to affirm that, with Christ, the profane in its "chemically" pure state had disappeared.[6]

This then is one of the positive aspects of the tendency perhaps improperly termed "desacralizing". It is not the happiest of terms; it can give rise to the suspicion that one is dealing with a negative activity whereas, on the contrary, attention is being called to a positive fact, a revolutionarily positive fact, the Christian fact, but called by way of a negation.

Without going into the matter too deeply, one might nonetheless mention a contemporary current of thought that is creating quite an effect and attracting much notice, the current of "de-religionizing". As it appears in its first and principal promoter, Dietrich Bonhöffer, a charismatic personality beyond question, it is manifestly a powerful reaction against so many Christians and theologians who split reality into two non-communicating sectors, the far vaster one of the profane and the diminutive, almost tangential, one of the cultic and sacral. Inasmuch as Bonhöffer imputes this vivisection to "religion" as distinct from Christianity (or as a force deforming Christianity), his campaign has been termed "de-religionizing". "I would like," he says, "to speak of God, placing him not at the circumference but at the center . . . How are we to speak of God in a lay manner, how are we to form a 'Church' without considering ourselves as set apart but rather as belonging fully to the world?" [7] "The opposition faith/religion pairs off with the opposition re-

---

[4] M.-D. Chenu, "The Laity and the 'Consecratio Mundi' " in La Iglesia del Vaticano II (Barcelona, 1966), pp. 999–1015.

[5] J. Grand'maison, Le sacré (Paris, 1966); P. Audet, "Le sacré et le profane. Leur situation en christianisme, in Nouv. Rev. Theol. 79 (1957), pp. 32–61; idem, "La revanche de Promethée," in Rev. Bibl. (1966), pp. 5–30; C. Geffré, "Desacralization and Sanctification," in Concilium 19 (1966), pp. 5–30.

[6] P. Teilhard de Chardin, Le milieu divin (Paris, 1957), p. 54.

[7] D. Bonhöffer, Widerstand und Ergebung; French tr.: Résistance et Soumission (Geneva, 1963), p. 123.

ligious/profane," says Geffré. "Religion introduces within human existence a dichotomy between the sacred and the profane,
while faith leaves to man his lay and worldly condition. Bonhöffer, with his opposition faith/religion, is trying to overcome
that of the sacred, taken in the narrow sense, and the profane,
taken in the pessimistic sense. Faith does not split human reality
into two halves, the sacred on one side and the profane on the
other, as if God took an interest solely in the sacred. By virtue
of the Gospel, everything has become sacred." [8] "This is the
essence of the religious perversion," says Robinson, "when worship becomes a realm into which to withdraw from the world,
to 'be with God'—even if it is only in order to receive strength
to go back into it. In this case the entire realm of the non-religious (in other words, 'life') is relegated to the profane, in the
strict sense of that which is outside the *fanum* or sanctuary. The
holy is that which is not common and which has to be taken from
the temple in order to sanctify the common . . . and we are
back at the Jewish priestly conception of the relation of the
sacred to the secular which was shattered by the Incarnation
when God declared all things holy. . . . Liturgy is . . . the
proclamation, the acknowledgment, the reception, the adoration,
of the holy in, with and under the common." [9]

For our part we must add that it would be wrong to think that
the liturgy is only that, a mere explicitation. It is indeed a sign,
a historical sign instituted by Christ. But within tradition the
notion of sign is bound up with that of efficaciousness. The sign
and the Word, both factors of explicitation, are the source from
which arises that which they signify and say. Liturgy does not
merely explicitate and proclaim the grace of Christ, it also brings
it forth, makes it present. Hence the privileged status of liturgical
action, qualitatively unique; hence the need to be specially em-
powered, to be given a *potestas* in order to preside over liturgical
acts (hierarchical priesthood).

Given these theological *a prioris,* factors of vivid experience

---

[8] C. Geffré, "La critique de la religion chez Barth et chez Bonhöffer,"
in *Parole et mission* 31 (1965), pp. 567–84.
[9] J. Robinson, *Honest to God* (London, 1963), pp. 86–88.

in a modern consciousness, the liturgy looks much closer to the life and reality that surround the Christian. It follows that the liturgical act in all its elements will have to appear not as something completely different but as something that maintains a continuity within a discontinuity with the daily life of the believer.

Now, what these theological *a prioris* tell us of the liturgy is abundantly confirmed by the very history and biblical foundation of the liturgy. The impact of Christianity on worship as a factor working against segregation and in that sense desacralizing, can be seen in the following elements: places, times, actions, persons.

The first point, that concerning the sacred place, is familiar enough. The text of Jesus' conversation with the Samaritan woman is quite explicit: "The hour is coming when men will adore the Father not on this mountain nor in Jerusalem . . . but in spirit and in truth" (Jn. 4, 21–24; 2, 19–21; Rom. 9, 6–13, 26–29; 11, 16–24). There is no preestablished localization of God, thanks to Jesus who has become Lord of the world, the firstborn of all creation, once and for all. A similar comment can be made concerning another decisive abolition made by the New Law, the abolition of the Sabbath (Mk. 2, 27–28). Just as there are for the Christian no particular sacred places, so there are for him no isolated and exclusive sacred times. The time properly termed "holy" is the "today", the "hour", the "day" inaugurated by Christ, that is to say, the time *post Christum* (Heb. 3, 7—4, 11). The Sabbath was no more than a shadow of the plenitude that has come with Christ (Col. 2, 16). This time, taken as a whole and not fragmented into isolated days, is called in Luke (4, 19–21) "the sabbatical year", the year of grace, of liberation from all servitudes, the year fulfilled in Christ, that is to say, realized in Christ. We can say with Rordorf: "The Sabbath as an institution and a sacred day disappears or is diffused throughout all days, throughout the every-day-ness of Christian experience. In this sense it is desacralized." [10] Today, little by little, we are beginning to take stock of certain passages

[10] W. Rordorf, *Der Sonntag* (Zurich, 1962), pp. 115–16.

in St. Paul, very strict and till now very much neglected, against those who go on "keeping" (let us say "setting apart") particular days: "You observe days, and months, and seasons, and years! I am afraid I have labored over you in vain" (Gal. 4, 10–11). "Let no one pass judgment on you in question of food and drink or with regard to festival or a moon or a sabbath. These are only a shadow of what is to come; but the substance belongs to Christ" (Col. 2, 16–17).

The New Testament idea is that all days are equal, not in the sense that they are all neutral but the reverse, in that they all form part of the "behold, now is the acceptable time" (2 Cor. 6, 1–10), inaugurated in Christ.

Within this all-levelling flood there does, however, stand out one day in the week, the first, the day of the Lord, the day of the resurrection, the glorification of Jesus. In what sense does it stand out? Not in that of remaining set apart for rest, since Christians worked on this day up till the 4th century; it stands out because on it they celebrate the Lord's supper; they come together for the eucharist. Now the Church from the earliest times did celebrate the eucharist on other days of the week, for example, in connection with the death of martyrs. Manifestly, therefore, not even Sunday is a day with an exclusive claim to the salvific intervention of God through the liturgy, the actualizing of his death and resurrection in the assembly of the faithful, that is, the Mass. From this it can be seen that every one of the days of the year is sacred history, can be sacred history, that is, the web woven of the interventions of God in the life of mankind, provided that Christians gather to celebrate the eucharist. Thus, although there is indeed a day in the week with a special status, the Sunday, that does not mean that the others cease to be capable of sanctification. (In this sense, there is a desacralization that stems from Christ.)

But the weightiest fact that we have to note in the first two centuries of Christianity is the absence of any festival other than the Sunday. Even the annual festival of Easter exists simply as the underlining of that particular weekly celebration of the resurrection that happened to coincide with the annual Jewish Pass-over, the anniversary of the death of Jesus.[11] They kept faith-fully to the spirit of St. Paul in not distinguishing anniversaries, special periods of the year (seasons), new moon festivals. In those centuries the year seems to be all on a level, like a lake with unbroken surface and whose waters cover all. Only little by little did there emerge, like islets, certain days observed with special festivity and which, linked one to the other, gradually form that solemn organic growth which we call today "the li-turgical year".

Now these festivals are in appearance absolutely alike in char-acter. They celebrate the same thing: the glorification of Jesus. Hence, every celebration finds its center in the eucharist. At first, none of these festivals, the Nativity, Holy Week or Pentecost, were meant to celebrate in isolation distinct stages of the life of Christ, his birth, his epiphany, Gethsemane, his ascension, the sending of the Spirit; they did not celebrate anniversaries, that is to say, they did not treat salvation history as a series of chrono-logically discrete moments.[12] The spirit recommended by St. Paul was kept. Origen states the matter very clearly (*Contra Celsum* VIII, 22): Christians have no need of festivals, unlike the pagans. Their whole life is a single festival, a Sunday, a Passover.[13] The loss of this spirit of sobriety—there are already signs of it in the 4th century—broke things down into fragments that in their turn demand a "defragmentation".

In all that refers to liturgical acts we may speak of a desacraliz-ing revision; thanks to the conciliar *Constitution on the Church*, we are recalled to the biblical doctrine that it is not only the liturgico-sacramental activity of the Christian that belongs to worship but also his life of charity, of apostolate, of prophetic

[11] J. A. Jungmann, "Das kirchliche Fest nach Idee und Granze," in *Liturgisches Erbe und pastorale Gegenwart* (Innsbruck, 1960), p. 527; C. Caliewärt, *Sacris erudiri* (Steenbruggen, 1940), p. 300.

[12] R. Cabie, *La Pentecôte* (Paris, 1960); R. Berger, "Ostern under Weihnachten," in *Archiv f. Litw.* 8 (1963), pp. 1–20; J. Mossay, "Noël et Epiphanie en Capadocie," in *Noël-Epiphanie retour du Christ* (Paris, 1966), p. 232.

[13] *G.C.S.* 2 (1899), pp. 239–40.

ministry (1 Pet. 2, 4–10; Rom. 15, 16, 17; 1, 4–10; Phil. 2, 17; 3, 3; 4, 18; Heb. 9, 4; 10, 22, 24; 12, 1; cf. *Constitution on the Church,* n. 34 and the *Decree on the Lay Apostolate,* n. 3).

The notion of worship remains also expanded and amplified. J. Frisque concludes: "This biblical and conciliar focus corresponds to the authentic anthropology of Christianity. If the category of worship is coterminous with the ritual, there is no valuation of Christian life in its religious dimension save insofar as it is studded with moments of explicit public worship, as if only thus could a given religious sentiment be achieved and apart from them the Christian life were deprived of it." [14]

"For a mentality like this," adds Hamman, "the religio-Christian is a mere addition to the profane; the liturgy is an *en-soi*. Things remain split into two compartments." [15]

Lastly, with respect to persons, let us remember that in the New Testament not only priests and pontiffs are sacred or holy persons but all the baptized. More than this, all men, insofar as they are brothers, are a sign of Christ (the neighbor as "sacrament").

These are the theologico-liturgical coordinates of the new spirit in which the new generations are emerging into the world of the liturgy. Other causes of the change might be specified, for example, the numerous laymen who see the presence of Christ in the facts of daily life, in the profane, etc.

One clear consequence for the composition of new formularies must be this; into them there must enter, with quite a new emphasis, a reference to temporal realities and to their character as signs of the times; they must show a quite special appreciation, based on faith, for all the so-called profane. They will also, each in its own way, have to form men to the contemplation of Christ as a dynamic salvific force not merely in the act of worship *sensu stricto* but also in that other worship *sensu analogico,* if you wish, but a sense nonetheless proper and real, the worship of

[14] J. Frisque, "Composants du 'culte' chrétien selon Vatican II," in *Paroisse et Liturgie* (1966), p. 612.

[15] A. Hamman, *Liturgie et Apostolat* (Paris, 1964), pp. 26–32.

the Christian's life as a whole. In this way passing from the profane to the sacred will not be a leap into the void but a smooth transition such as is demanded by contemporary theology.[16]

[16] *Paroisse et Liturgie* (1967), pp. 241–42. The Dutch formulary published here was of great interest to a number of priests of different South American nationalities, who studied it in a course of liturgy. But on the other hand the anaphora published by Dom Vagaggini in *Il canone della messa e la riforma liturgica* (Turin, 1966), pp. 100–113 and printed in *Paroisse et Liturgie* (1967), p. 229, aroused no interest in them, although they recognized its formal values. Quite apart from the criticisms made of it by Jungmann in *Liturgisches Jahrbuch* 17 (1967), pp. 1–18, they found it outworn. Its ideas move in a religious "Olympus" without any reflection in the concrete life of modern man with all its values both real and mistaken, its light and shade, fears and hopes. In today's creation of new texts it is not enough to copy the old ones, eliminating simply certain formal imperfections. That would be archaism. Things being so, it is clear that new texts cannot be produced by any single supreme organ, however international the composition of its membership. It is urgently necessary to pass on to local Churches the right not only of translating but also of composing formularies. New ideas on this theme are to be found in the work of G. Gamber, *Liturgie ubermorgen. Gedanken zur Geschichte und Zukunft des Gottesdienstes* (Freiburg im Br., 1966).

Theodore Stone/*Chicago, Illinois*
Sister Anselm Cunningham, O.P./*Urbana, Illinois*

The Chicago Experimental Funeral Rite

I n September, 1966, the Liturgical Commission of the Archdiocese of Chicago established a working committee to study the problem of parochial funerals in relation to article 81 of the *Constitution on the Sacred Liturgy*: "The rite for the burial of the dead should express more clearly the paschal character of Christian death." At that time only the Archdioceses of St. Louis and Atlanta in the United States had permission to use an experimental funeral rite.

In examining the experiments in Atlanta and St. Louis, the Chicago study committee felt the paschal character of Christian death was not sufficiently emphasized. A recent article in *Worship*[1] corroborates this judgment and describes the Atlanta and St. Louis experiments as valid efforts at improvement but unimaginative and uncreative. Study reveals that the rites are verbatim renderings received from the post-conciliar Commission on the Liturgy. The Roman document on the funeral rite is a *ritus typicus* and as such it offers guidelines, not hard and fast directives. No doubt there are limitations in experimenting with a rite developed by experts on one side of the world for exposure in parishes all over the globe—but the invitation to alter and to substitute seem, in the Atlanta and St. Louis instances at least, not to have been seized upon as completely as possible.

---

[1] Aelred Tegels, "The New Funeral Rites", *Worship* XL (December, 1966), pp. 658–61.

99

I

General Principles for the Experiment

A further invitation to liturgical creativity has been extended in a series of general principles and introductory directives for the experiment. These first appeared in *Notitiae*[2] for December, 1966, and were translated into English for the *Newsletter* of the Bishops' Commission on the Liturgical Apostolate,[3] January, 1967.

The description in *Notitiae* is written by Father Pierre-Marie Gy, O.P., and begins with a general statement of the problem: the already wide variety of customary usages at funeral services and the will of the Council that funerals "should express more clearly the paschal character of Christian death and should correspond more closely to the circumstances and traditions found in various regions".

This basic variety of funeral services goes all the way from the full rite which is celebrated in three stages (the home of the dead person, the church, and the cemetery) to the service which, in some countries, is limited strictly to the home of the dead person.

The development of an improved Roman rite for funerals is, of course, only the first step since the preparation of particular (especially national) rituals was left by the Council to the episcopal conferences (Constitution, Art. 63b). The core rite, which is the subject of the present experiment, is planned for ultimate inclusion in the Roman Ritual. Even in its tentative form it tries to allow for diversity of practice; for example:

1. All the liturgical texts (prayers, chants) are arranged so that others may be substituted, according to circumstances. This is intended to achieve greater appropriateness and authenticity.

2. Some elements or parts of the rite are left open to free in-

[2] *Notitiae* is the report series issued by the Consilium for the implementation of the *Constitution on the Sacred Liturgy* (post-conciliar Liturgical Commission).

[3] Bishops' Commission on the Liturgical Apostolate *Newsletter* III (January, 1967), pp. 1–3.

clusion or omission, as conditions dictate. For example, a single prayer may be provided in the text, but a note will be added to suggest the possible addition of a psalm or a second prayer, as desired.

3. The pastoral difficulty in using some of the psalms is recognized, so that alternatives are provided, as well as a special rule allowing for the omission of one or other verse which may be poorly understood.

The new texts of prayers are generally those taken from existing sources, so that they will harmonize with the existing prayers which have been retained or slightly modified. A good number of options have been added, and existing texts have been suppressed if they are in conflict with the sense of Christian hope.

One expectation of the Consilium is that Latin texts which may be inexact theologically (for example, in responsories) may be corrected or improved in translation.

One final point is made in the *Notitiae* description of the experiment, that the texts in the rite may serve as examples so that, in local rituals, the episcopal conferences may substitute prayers of original composition.

One individual question concerns the adaptation of rites like incensations and sprinklings with holy water. Cultural traditions may suggest the retention or introduction of these practices, their omission, or the study of possible substitute rites. Another example is the liturgical color for funeral services, a change proposed by the Council (Constitution, Art. 81). In the experiment different colors may be chosen; when the results of the experiment have been studied, the matter, according to the Consilium's proposal, will be left to the episcopal conferences.

II

EDUCATIONAL PREPARATION PROGRAM AND EVALUATION

It is in this light of this creative experimentation that the "Chicago rite" has been prepared. Those working with the proposed rite are hopeful that other dioceses now permitted to expand liturgical experimentation will make use of the Chicago documents to their advantage. Essential to the implementation of the ritual are the educational preparation program and the subsequent evaluation plan. While the former is sound pedagogy, the latter is integral to further adaptation and use.[4]

Since the educational program needs to precede the actual use of the rite, the Chicago adaptation has not yet been used. Even when permission is given, its use before early 1968 is not contemplated because of the felt importance of sound educational preparation. Envisioned for the education of the diocese in this regard are a series of study days built around the theology of Christian death. The study days include priests, Sister coordinators of parish liturgy, funeral directors, and the parish lectors and commentators, usually laymen. Position papers on "The Paschal Mystery and Death" and "The American View of Death and Life" have been prepared for all participants. A twenty-thirty minute color film will also be commercially prepared which will describe the experimental rite, attempting to work out creatively the rich symbolism involved in the rite itself. It is hoped that the film will lend itself to television presentation and to viewing in dioceses throughout the country.

Those parishes in the Archdiocese of Chicago that wish to use the rite and fulfill the basic requirements will be involved in further study programs and the evaluation program. Chicago is fortunate in having professional agencies such as the National Opinion Research Center and local Catholic universities such as Loyola University. It is hoped that personnel from such agencies will guide the evaluation of the project. Progress reports and all results of the evaluation will be sent to the Bishops' Commission on the Liturgical Apostolate for their study and recommendations.

[4] Bishops' Commission on the Liturgical Apostolate *Newsletter* III (February, 1967), p. 4.

III

DESCRIPTION OF THE CHICAGO EXPERIMENTAL RITE

The following is a skeleton outline of the Chicago experimental rite. In Chicago, custom calls for a funeral Mass and a service at the cemetery, and presumes that the parish priest will attend the wake. The proposed Ritual has been divided according to this threefold aspect: Wake Service, Service at the Church and Cemetery Service.

Some basic considerations must be made. Such a rite should be cognizant that a harmonious balance must be struck between the human sorrow and grief of the bereaved in their loss and the quality of consolation that must be offered them in the light of Christ's promise of the resurrection. The Chicago rite attempts to emphasize the latter, while respecting the human needs of the mourners.

Unnecessary duplication of signs or prayers has been avoided. The educational program will attempt to guide the priests to steer clear of such duplication (exercising certain options) unless pastoral reasons urge otherwise.

A vigilant attempt has been made to so structure the rite that it moves toward a climax, from the vigil beginning with recognition of sorrow and loss, then to the meeting of the body at the door of the church reminiscent of the day of baptism, then to the eucharistic liturgy to relate the eucharist to the death and life of the Christian, then to the final commendation as a fitting prelude to the procession from the church marking the triumph over death, and finally to the ceremony at the cemetery at which the mourners look forward to final resurrection and parousia.

The Wake Service

The vigil at the wake is a communal service consisting of readings and prayers. Copies of the service in throwaway form ought to be distributed at the funeral parlor. The priest is usually dressed in civilian garb and wears a small stole—violet is recommended in sympathy with the sorrow of the mourners and as a prelude to the white to be worn at the funeral Mass. The priest may invite a layman to join in the proclamation of the Word of God in the readings. Suggested for the wake service are readings from: Ezechiel 37, 12–14; Apocalypse 21, 2–5 and John 16, 20–22, although the priest may substitute other readings than those listed when he so desires. Responsory psalms are interspersed. Suggested are: Psalm 129 with a refrain and Psalm 50, 1–7, 12–14. A homily on the scripture readings in relation to Christian death is recommended along with a recitation of the Lord's Prayer and a Prayer of the Faithful.[5]

The Church Service

The ceremony of meeting the body at the door of the church includes the use of those symbols that are reminders of the baptism of the Christian: holy water, white pall, paschal candle. It is here that the simplicity and richness of the rite is overwhelmingly evident in the focusing of attention on the essential, primordial symbols of our personal participation in the paschal mystery.

The procession to meet the body is led by servers, one carrying a processional cross, another the paschal candle. Vested in white chasuble the priest goes to the door of the church to meet the funeral cortege. The celebrant then sprinkles the casket with holy water.

I bless you, N. with the holy water that recalls the day of your re-birth in the living waters of baptism, that day of which St. Paul has written: "When we were baptized in Christ Jesus we were baptized in his death; in other words, when we were baptized, we went into the tomb with him and joined him in death, so that as Christ was raised from the dead by the Father's glory, we too might live a new life. If in union with Christ we have imitated his death, we shall also imitate him in his resurrection."

(Rom. 6, 3–5)

[5] The Roman Document calls for a homily (#12), The Lord's Prayer (#13) and the Prayer of the Faithful (#117).

Following this while still in the vestibule a white pall, completely covering the casket, reminiscent of the white baptismal robe and decorated with symbols of the risen Christ, is placed on the casket by the pallbearers.

The true meaning of the Introit of the Mass is restored in this context as the entrance processional since it is recited or sung as the cross, paschal candle, servers and celebrant leads the procession to the altar.

In the Mass, the use of white vestments is essential to the experiment—to relate the death of the Christian to his baptism and to capture the note of Christ's triumph over death. The celebrant is free to choose any of the ten epistles and ten gospels in any translation approved for liturgical use or to substitute even a different reading whenever an alternate one would serve the occasion better. The Liturgical Commission of the Archdiocese of Chicago has prepared a lectionary with the proper chants, epistle and gospel selections and alternate proper parts.

A collection of coordinated *prayers of the assembly, prayers over the gifts and prayers after communion,* have been prepared for particular instances such as "In Case of a Sudden Death":

Collect
O God, whose gifts to men are always generous and spontaneous, we gather today to ask you, in the name of your Son, to receive *N.* into the glory of your kingdom as you have promised all who believe in you. Through Jesus Christ. . . .

Prayer over the Gifts
Accept, O Father, these gifts in the name of your Son, whose resurrection gives us hope. May the suddenness of *N.'s* death be a sign of your spontaneous gifts to all of us. Through Jesus Christ. . . .

or "For a Religious Sister":

Collect

O God, who gives eternal life to those who love you, look with kindness upon those who profess their love for you, and especially upon *N.,* your daughter, whose life with her sisters was a sign of her love for you. Through Jesus Christ. . . .

or "For the Father of a Family":

Collect

O God, our ever-loving Father, we gather today to remember *N.* an earthly father of your children. May his care for his family be a sign of your eternal care for all of us. Through Jesus Christ. . . .

In keeping with the paschal character of the Mass, a gradual and alleluia verse will be recited or sung. The tract and sequence (*Dies Irae*) are eliminated.

The homily is obligatory, not optional and it is not to be a eulogy. With the choice of lessons, the homily offers many more opportunities for diversity in presenting and applying God's message on the meaning of death and eternal life.

A noteworthy change in ceremony within the Mass is the rite of incensation at the offertory and the elimination of it in the rite after Mass to avoid unnecessary duplication. The former "Absolution" is now, in accord with the Roman document, called the "Final Commendation". A responsory and introductory prayer used in the Chicago rite are taken directly from the Roman document #117. A simple litany expressive of the better sentiments in the *Libera* (now eliminated) but better relating our "deliverance" to the power of Christ's mysteries is included.

The procession to the cemetery (i.e., the portion of it that takes place in the church) is to be led by the cross and the paschal candle. This symbol of Christ triumphing over death, sin and the grave is reminiscent of our symbolic triumph through darkness to light on Holy Saturday.

The Cemetery Service

The gospel reading (John 14, 1–6; John 12, 23–26; John 17, 24–26 or Apocalypse 21, 2–5), psalms (e.g., 22, 26, 41, 102, 113, 114, 129), responsory and refrain used here are chosen to reflect the reunion of the deceased with the risen Christ forever. There is, therefore, less emphasis, on the element of human sorrow and considerably more on the true joy that the death of a good Christian engenders in the hearts of those who "lose" him for a time only—and only to God. This notion of farewell is borrowed from pagan usage because it is a profoundly human act. It is not only a farewell from the community but a "commendation". The cemetery service or committal or farewell rite, suppresses the *Benedictus* canticle and proposes a brief litany, with the Lord's Prayer recited by all as the conclusion.

Heinrich Rennings / *Trier, W. Germany*

Spotlight on the Reform of the Funeral Rite

The fears of many a pessimist have proved to be unfounded: the liturgy is not being reformed behind closed doors by a few experts. While in the 1950's the liturgical reforms were worked out in private at the desk of some liturgical experts and then presented to a clergy and laity who were grateful yet taken by surprise, the Commission for the execution of the *Constitution on the Sacred Liturgy* has made a serious effort to spread information. This is in fact the only way to make this reform involve the whole Church, as Cardinal Lercaro, the President of the Consilium, said it should be in his letter to the Chairmen of the National Episcopal Conferences of June 30, 1965. If, in spite of this, justified expectation of more punctual and detailed information has still remained unfulfilled on many points, the blame does not lie with a lack of goodwill in the Consilium but rather with the conditions in which it must work within the Roman Curia. So even the members of the Consilium often do not know what alterations will be made in an agreed text before publication.

The *Notitiae*, the monthly publication of the Consilium, already published in December 1966,[1] for general information, an extensive description of the new burial rite for adults. The

[1] *Notitiae* 2 (1966), pp. 353–63; cf. the excerpts in the article by T. Stone and A. Cunningham in this issue of *Concilium*.

outline of this rite was prepared by the French Dominican, Fr.
P. M. Gy, who leads Study Group 23.[2] Contrary to the opinion
that there should be no public exchange of views on the rites
that were introduced *ad experimentum* during the testing period,
the *Notitiae* reported on a few initial experiments.[3]

Should Adjustment Be Based Only on Selection?

One of the principles laid down by the *Constitution on the
Sacred Liturgy* demanded that the rites should be adapted to
"the people's powers of comprehension" (Art. 34). Now, this
power of comprehension varies a great deal according to age,
milieu, conditions of life and degree of understanding of the
faith (cf. Art. 19). If we take such varied circumstances into
consideration there can be no rigidly uniform rite. Apart from
this adjustment to individual circumstances the conciliar text
explicitly demands that the rites be adjusted to the various liturgical communities, the customs and character of different regions and peoples (cf. Art. 37f.). This requires again a necessary elasticity in the liturgical regulations, directives for which
are contained in articles 39 and 40 of the Constitution.

The project for the burial rite meets these requirements by
offering a number of variations. Thus, for instance, it provides
for three general basic forms. The first mentions three places for
the liturgical gathering (the home of the dead person, the church
and the cemetery); the second foresees only two: the cemetery
chapel and the grave, while the third mentions only one single
rite, and this in the home of the dead person. Each of these
three basic forms contains a wide choice of prayers, psalms,
readings, antiphons, etc. The brief rubric "vel" or "ad libitum
alia"—so frequent in the old liturgical books and so rare in the
Tridentine reform—creates a considerable flexibility in the rite.

The question nevertheless arises, whether the mere choice
from among a number of formularies in the Roman Ritual is
enough to ensure that the liturgy corresponds to a given concrete

[2] P. Gy also wrote the chapter, "The Death of the Christian," in
L'Eglise en prière.
[3] *Notitiae* 2 (1966), p. 363; 3 (1967), pp. 155–64.

situation. Those who drafted the burial rite "ad experimentum" do not think so. The report in the *Notitiae* explicitly mentions[4] that the episcopal conferences can adopt new texts for the burial rites of the regional rituals, texts that are not contained in the model rite given in the Roman Ritual. If these texts of the Roman Ritual are said to be the model for the special texts of the Rituals of the local Churches this does not mean that the regional texts should be a mere imitation of the model; the character of "model text" of a new Roman Ritual should be seen to lie rather in the way it tries to put into practice the basic principles of the Constitution. It is therefore possible—and in many cases necessary—that a regional ritual will have nothing in common with the new rite of the Roman Ritual except the spirit and principles of the liturgical renewal.

It is therefore already very doubtful whether such a use of the opportunities offered by the Council will suffice to bring about a genuine accordance between the liturgical regulations and the given situation of a burial, particularly with regard to the prayers. Whether these texts are those of the Roman Ritual or of a regional ritual, in both cases the adaptation to the given situation is limited to a choice from an already existing collection of prayers. This is no doubt already an acceptable enrichment, not to be underrated, since it goes well beyond what the present Roman Ritual has to offer, which is only a small choice of prayers that can be suited to the occasion.[5] But can we really expect an established collection of texts to contain models for every situation? Judging from his experience of a large number of prayer formulas used for burial in the Evangelical Church, F. Schulz

---

[4] *Loc. cit.*, p. 356.

[5] For instance in the *Office of the Dead* (Tit. VII, Cap. IV). The prayer varies according to whether it is used for the 3rd, 7th or 30th day after the burial or for the anniversary. Significant of the clerical and hierarchical character of the liturgy were the variations in the text according to the dead person: 9 variations for a cleric (for a pope, a bishop, a cardinal-bishop, a cardinal-priest endowed with episcopal dignity, for a cardinal-priest not so endowed, for a cardinal-deacon who was a priest, for a cardinal-deacon who was not ordained priest, for a dead priest, and others); the laity only knows a dead person, brothers, relatives and benefactors, father and mother.

says: "The justified wish to bring the specific situation into the prayers is not satisfied by a vast number of prayers for categories of cases (which never quite fit), but by the preacher using a prepared but free prayer of his own."[6] Such a collection of prayers then serves the purpose of showing how a personal prayer should run, and occasionally one of the models can of course be taken over verbally. There is, however, no obligation to use the model texts. It is up to the celebrant to understand the given particular situation and to bring it into his prayer, with due respect for the character of official ecclesiastical liturgical prayer.

The spread of the liturgical renewal in the Catholic Church will have to consider sooner or later similar solutions in its concern for bringing the liturgy into harmony with the given situation. In any case this presupposes celebrants who are properly trained and capable of handling this problem. But if we expect a priest to compose his own sermon, is it not possible that we shall sometime have a generation of clergy who can compose a liturgical prayer?

Psalms and Hymns

The draft of the new burial rite frequently mentions the singing of psalms. The abundant use of the psalms is justified by the statement that "after the eucharistic sacrifice the Church has nothing holier than the prayer of the psalms, nothing more suitable to express grief, and nothing more effective to strengthen hope".[7] Even if one sees in this a certain rhetorical exaggeration, there is also the danger of wanting to find a theory for an exaggerated use of psalms.[8] The rubrics of the new rite, which

[6] F. Schulz, "Die evangelischen Begräbnisgebete des 16. und 17. Jahrhunderts," in *Jahrbuch für Liturgik und Hymnologie* 11 (1966), p. 1.

[7] *Notitiae* 3 (1967), p. 164.

[8] In the introduction to *Begräbnisagende* (Kassel 1962), which he published together with the *Evangelische Michaelsbruderschaft*, W. Lotz referred to his experiences in German Protestantism and expressed the opinion: "The question of psalms sung or said alternately is practically never raised in connection with a burial." Nevertheless, Lotz could not do wholly without the psalms.

allow a change in the psalms and the omission of certain pastorally less appropriate verses, are welcome and helpful, but do not solve the problem. The problem is that the funeral rite should not be limited to psalms for the sung parts but should leave room for the whole wealth of liturgical texts, liturgical chant and even for purely instrumental music. When one has heard a choir and community, standing by the open grave, sing: "O Sacred Head, sore wounded" (with the verse: "When once I must depart, depart thou not from me; when I suffer death, be thou present. When my heart is pressed with fear, let thy fear and pain deliver me"), one has to admit that in a liturgy for men of this age and from all countries the psalms must yield sometimes to texts that are more immediately appealing than those used by the people of the Old Covenant.[9]

The Instruction on "Music in the Liturgy," of March 5, 1967, expects that, for the liturgy of the sacraments and sacramentals, "appropriate music will be available in order to make a more solemn celebration possible in the vernacular" (n. 45). On such occasions one should also think of instrumental music (nn. 62–7).[10] A uniform rite for the whole Latin Church can obviously not give any indications on this point. That is the business of the local rituals. One might wonder, though, whether the Roman Ritual, too, should not foresee such possibilities in its model rites for a burial, if it cares to forestall the objection that it is only concerned with a one-sided concentration on psalms and shows an a-musical mentality. Instead of, or along with, a list of more and more psalms there should be a brief exposé of the function and character of the sung parts (cf. the Instruction on Music of March 5, 1967, n. 6) so that those who have to

[9] This wish is also mentioned in a report on an experimental use of the new project from London (Canada); see *Notitiae* 3 (1967), p. 164.

[10] The prohibition of purely instrumental music at the office of the dead and the Mass for the dead (not the burial rite as such), contained in n. 66 of the Instruction, is difficult to reconcile with Art. 120 of the Constitution which leaves such decisions to the episcopal conference. Moreover, this prohibition is based on a lack of appreciation of the function of instrumental music in the liturgy.

draft the rituals for the local Churches would have some indica-
tion to guide them in their adaptation to local needs.

The Availability of a Properly Equipped Congregation

Quite rightly, the new liturgical regulations were planned in
terms of a worshipping community whose members would be
capable of filling certain roles. Now the primary roles necessary
to the conduct of liturgical celebration are those of celebrant,
cantors and readers, and a congregation capable of actual participation. The new burial rite allocates certain duties to each
of these roles so the implementation of the new rite is naturally
dependent upon the existence in the community of people able
to carry them out. Without this no Christian congregation can
celebrate in the spirit of the liturgical renewal. If, therefore, there
are still many congregations today that are not yet able to play
their full part, it is clearly urgent for those in charge to train
these congregations up to the required standard. It would be no
solution to lay down fresh liturgical regulations based on a situation where the congregation is incapable of taking an active part
in the liturgy.

Insofar as the funeral rite is concerned there is a special problem here. The experimental draft itself points out that people
are often present at the liturgical celebration of a burial, who
are either non-Catholics or Catholics who rarely or never come
to Mass or seem to have lost the faith altogether. It frequently
occurs in many countries that on such occasions the congregation consists for a large part or almost exclusively of people who
do not go to church. In such a case no such organized participation is possible. Active participation is extremely limited when
the congregation cannot even say the Our Father together. The
inability of those present to share in the alternated prayers, the
dialogue, the salutations, intercession, antiphons, responsories,
etc., rules out a liturgical organization which rests on such a
participation.[11] One has to agree with W. Lotz when he says:

[11] This differs from the situation at a funeral service where a Christian
congregation is present. In that case, the "outsider" (non-Catholic or

"One cannot use religious formulas and gestures that might strike those present as a strange flowery language or as a liturgy that is forced down their throat." [12] This creates the problem of a liturgy that must do without important executants, perhaps even without all of them except the celebrant. This situation is not exactly new. It was common in many services before the renewal of the liturgy. What is new, however, is that the way this problem was solved in the past is no longer acceptable. It simply consisted in letting the celebrant, and perhaps one assistant, take over all the functions that would otherwise be left out. If one, for sound reasons, holds that such an accumulation of various functions on one person[13] is incompatible with the spirit of the liturgical Constitution, the only solution seems to lie in drafting a burial rite which requires only one executant to be actually present. The Order of Burial for an Adult provides some material for this but one has the impression that the problem has not been taken properly into account. The "missionary" responsibility of the celebrant at such a burial service cannot find adequate expression only in the sermon (which must be preaching to non-Catholics and catechumens), but also in the rite as a whole.

The Link between Tradition and the Present

The description of the funeral rite in the *Notitiae* states that for the text of the prayers, readings and sung pieces those have been generally kept that occurred already in the liturgical books of the Roman rite, with some minor alterations and some additions from older liturgical sources.[14] This procedure might be justified by referring to the liturgical Constitution where it says that the new forms should be organically developed from the

---

lapsed Catholic) knows that he is present as a stranger at an intimate celebration, of which he may not understand the style and customs but which he will nevertheless respect as a guest.

[12] *Loc. cit.*, p. 6.

[13] An extreme case of this accumulation is the eucharistic celebration by one priest without even an altar server, by papal indult.

[14] *Notitiae* 2 (1966), p. 355.

existing ones (Art. 23). One may, however, wonder whether this, no doubt necessary, link with the past is best preserved by simply using traditional texts. These texts were once composed or chosen (from the Bible) because they expressed the reality of the faith for the people of those days in a way they could understand. Is this continuity of tradition not better served by using the same criterion applied by tradition itself than by simply using old texts? If so, the criterion would be: Do the texts of a renewed liturgy bring modern man closer to these realities of the faith or do they cut him off? Do they express his Christian experience, his feelings, his thought, his hope? The unchangeability of the reality of the faith by no means needs to be expressed in unchangeable texts. This difficult task of working out new texts cannot be wholly left to those that draft the regional rituals. For the Roman Ritual should not show them how the people prayed in the Latin rite of the past but how they pray today. The better this task is fulfilled in the models of the Roman Ritual itself (not based merely on liturgiology but rather on contemporary spirituality), the more we can hope that the new Ritual will not remain a mere fruit of scholarly application but will be an inspiration for the local Churches. Thus the "substantial unity" of the Roman rite mentioned in the Constitution, Art. 38, has a chance of being maintained.

PART II
BIBLIOGRAPHICAL
SURVEY

Helmut Hucke/*Neu Isenburg, W. Germany*

The Roman Instruction on Music in the Liturgy

The Instruction *Musicam Sacram* was published on *Laetare* Sunday, March 5, 1967.

It is now known that this Instruction had a difficult birth. The first draft was presented in February, 1965,[1] and the *Consilium ad exsequendam Constitutionem de Sacra Liturgia* rejected a fifth draft on December 2, 1965, after intensive consultations which continued almost for a whole year.[2] "It soon became known that certain influential Church musicians and consultants to the council of bishops, who eventually did no longer cooperate, had objected in various high quarters that the musical heritage in the Latin language was in danger of falling into neglect." [3] More than a year passed before the Instruction was finally published.

[1] *Rinnovamento liturgico e Musica sacra.* Commento alla Istruzione 'Musicam Sacram'. Bibliotheca *Ephemerides Liturgicae*, Sectio pastoralis, IV, p. 42.

[2] E. J. Lengeling, "Zur neuen Instruktion über die 'Kirchenmusik innerhalb der Liturgie', in *Bibel und Liturgie*, 40 (1967), p. 184.

[3] E. J. Lengeling, *ibid.* "At hoc tempore non defuerunt voces contentiosae, ope aliquorum diariorum aut unius alteriusve consociationis propalatae, quae dubia moverent de interpretatione Constitutionis, timores urgerent circa possibilem deperditionem thesauri musicae sacrae e superioribus saeculis traditi; damna conclamarent insurgentia e derelictione linguae latinae et cantus gregorianae" (roughly translated in the text), in *Rinnovamento* etc., p. 42. Between the start on the work for the Instruction and its publication two international Congresses on Church

119

Almost all commentators have pointed out that the text was incoherent and that some abrupt transitions, differences in style and terminology in various sections, certain contradictions in the text and an appeal to pre-conciliar ordinances showed up subsequent interpolations, particularly in articles 4a, 4b and 28. These interpolations were naturally interpreted in the light of the conflicts which preceded the publication of the document. Hence the Instruction has been commented upon with frank disappointment or merely ignored by the commentators. On the one hand it is said that, basically, it has not said anything new, while on the other, it was hopefully thought that nothing had changed and everything has remained as before.

The general view is that progressive and conservative tendencies have been allowed to cancel each other out or at least been reduced to a neutral attitude. The result is that it is taken to be a painful attempt to confirm the Instruction on Church Music of the Congregation of Rites in 1958, while adjusting it more or less reluctantly to the conciliar *Constitution on the Sacred Liturgy*. And so the new Instruction is said to be a disappointing and even disturbing document insofar as the reform of the liturgy is concerned, or as a proof that the traditional positions have been reinforced and that sacred music has been on the right path already for a very long time.

A few commentators, however, take a different view. They see the Instruction as marking a new phase in the reform of the

music took place: in Freiburg (Switzerland), August 1965, an International Study Week on singing in the liturgy, and in Milwaukee and Chicago, August 1966, a Congress of the Consociatio Internationalis Musicae Sacrae. The papers of the Freiburg Study Week have been published in several languages: *Kirchenmusik nach dem Konzil* (Freiburg, Breisgau, 1967); *Le chant liturgique après Vatican II*. Kinnor, vol. VI (Paris, 1966); "La Musica nel rinnovamento liturgicao," in *Liturgia e cultura*, vol. II (Turin, 1966). The papers of the American Congress have not yet appeared. The President of the Consociatio, Prof. Dr J. Overath (Cologne), used this occasion to give incorrect information to the press, as a result of which the international society "Universa laus" for singing and music in the liturgy, an offspring of the Freiburg Study Week, was condemned by the Holy See. The *Consilium ad exsequendam Constitutionem de Sacra Liturgia* was authorized to amend this calumny and published an explanation in *Notitiae*, 21–22 (1966), p. 249.

liturgy, and even as the most forward-looking among the various practical directives that followed the *Constitution on the Sacred Liturgy*.[4] These commentators are not so much concerned with particular rules and regulations in the text as with the underlying principles and the general concept that emerges from them.

In fact, the disappointment with the Instruction seems to be based ultimately on the fact that the basic change of approach is overlooked which separates it from the pre-conciliar regulations on Church music. What the text contains in matters beyond juridical statements was seen as basically mere "stuffing" and decoration. The historical, aesthetic and theoretical views on musical problems were considered by musicians mainly as part of the curial style of the text, not as concrete statements to be taken seriously. And so these views were glossed over and people looked for firm decisions about what was and was not allowed. But a careful reading of the Instruction shows that the emphasis has changed in this document, and that the real content is concerned with statements of principle, not with rubrics. On this point alone the Instruction must already be accepted as a forward-looking document for the reform of the liturgy. The more deeply one penetrates into the text, the more one realizes that the Instruction means precisely to avoid the rubric approach and to lay down general principles. The preface states explicitly that the text does not intend to be a summary of the Church's legislation on Church music but merely to lay down "particularly significant directives which seem urgently required at the present time".[5] The concrete statements in one or other direction bear the stamp of useful applications rather than of rubrics. They are an attempt at clarifying the basic principles and their realization in the celebrating community.

The effect of the subsequent interpolations which the text suffered between the rejection by the Consilium and the date of publication, and which it would be futile to argue with or to ex-

[4] Cf. *Rinnovamento* etc., and the commentaries which appeared in such periodicals as *Musik und Altar, Eglise qui chante* and *Il Canto dell'Assemblea*.

[5] Art. 3.

plain away, was that the main lines of the document were obscured since these alterations laced the Instruction throughout with elements of rubricism. Precisely because of this rubricism it is clear that these interpolations did not really affect the true content, principles and basic statements.

The Pre-Conciliar Idea of Sacred Music

The title of the Instruction is *Instructio de Musica in Sacra Liturgia*. Comparison of this title with that of the Instruction of 1958, which was *De Musica Sacra et Sacra Liturgia,* shows already a basically different approach from that of previous ordinances about Church music: music and liturgy are no longer seen as two separate concerns. The new title avoids the phrase *musica sacra* altogether and it is only used reluctantly and in a narrow sense in the text.

To describe singing and making music in church as "sacred music" is not a usage of long standing.[6] The expression derives from German Lutheranism and originally referred to religious music in the broader sense, as opposed to "Church music". The Romantic period saw the ideal of sacred music in the *a cappella* style of the old Italians. This ideal and this style were taken by the movement for renewal of Church music in the second half of the 19th century as expressed in the "Roman polyphony" of the 16th century, and supporters made this type of sacred music their program in opposition to a musical practice that had lost the link with musical art as well as with the liturgy by accommodating itself to the new kind of bourgeois entertainment and *salon* music of those days. They plagiarized the style and the repertory from *Wedding March* to *Valse Triste* in order to produce religious emotions.

When Pius X, in his Motu proprio of 1903, used the title "Instruction on Sacred Music" he therefore identified Church music with this program kind of *musica sacra*. At the same time, however, he explicitly guided the renewal of Church music toward plain chant as "the chant of the Roman Church" and "the noblest example of sacred music".

[6] Cf. *Rinnovamento* etc., pp. 56–60.

Sacred music in the proper sense then still meant the repertory and practice of polyphony in Church choirs. Even Pius XI still spoke of sacred music and plain chant as two different things.[7] In order to separate sacred music from the current abuses in Church music, it was defined as having to be holy, and far from all that is profane. It must have the character of true art, "because otherwise it cannot exercise that influence on those that hear it, which the Church implies when it integrates the art of music into the liturgy".[8] This concept of sacred music as the artistic achievement of Church choirs explains the maxim that it must be "the humble servant of the liturgy". This also explains why sacred music is understood as mere "decoration", an "essential part", it is true, but only of the "solemn liturgy".[9] The point of Pius X's Motu proprio is not singing in the liturgy, but the "sacred music" of Church choirs and the conditions on which it is allowed in liturgical celebrations. That is why this "general code of sacred music" does not deal with the singing of priests and ministers, and that the only singing by the congregation mentioned is taking part in plain chant.

Official statements during the pontificate of Pius XII tried on the one hand to keep abreast of artistic developments in the *musica sacra* and on the other, to accommodate the problems raised by the liturgical movement. This was done by extending the notion of "sacred music" beyond its earlier content and by somehow bringing it under the control of rubrics with the help of the principles laid down by Pius X, which principles thereby assumed a very different character. Typical of this procedure is the listing of various "kinds" of sacred music. Pius X had, in his Motu proprio, pointed to plain chant as the ideal, an ideal with which the classic polyphony of the Roman School of the 16th century was closely connected. But modern music, too, had produced works of art that were not unworthy of the liturgical

---

[7] In the title of the Apostolic Constitution *Divini Cultus*, of Dec. 20, 1928: *De liturgia deque cantu gregoriano et musica sacra cotidie magis provehendis.*

[8] Art. 2.

[9] Art. 1.

celebration.[10] The Instruction of the Congregation of Rites, of 1958, then distinguished three kinds of sacred music. The first was plain chant, defined as the music which is incorporated in the liturgical books. The second was called "sacred polyphony" and embraced the period between plain chant and the maturity of classic polyphony of the 16th century. On the basis of what Pius X said about more modern music, the third kind is called "modern sacred music" and this term covered the music composed for use in the liturgy after the 16th century, but this referred only to "polyphony" as understood by Pius X. To these three kinds three others were added, namely, sacred music for the organ, popular religious chant and religious music at large;[11] the last two items included by definition all non-Christian religious singing and music-making.[12] Together, these six kinds of sacred music represent all kinds of categories: juridical, historical, practical, sociological and spiritual. All that they have really in common is that they can all be incorporated in the musical repertoire.

Church music must obviously have a musical repertoire, but such an identification of the repertoire with Church music at large, and the idea that such a repertoire constitutes liturgical music as such, become impossible when we understand by liturgical celebration something that is happening, something that implies action. Even from the musical and artistic point of view this is untenable, for such a view corresponds in no way to the demands of music as an art, as the defenders of the *musica sacra* pretend, and is still less aware of Church music as a true art. It is rather a statement in defense of a peculiar cultural attitude which is alien to contemporary music, and, *au fond,* artistically irrelevant.

Singing as Part of the Liturgical Action

In his Motu proprio Pius X pointed to plain chant as the exemplar of sacred music: "A composition is the more ecclesial

10 Art. 3–5.
11 Art. 4–10.
12 Art. 9–10.

and liturgical as it approaches plain chant in design, spirit and mood." [13] Over against this, the *Constitution on the Sacred Liturgy* says: "Therefore sacred music is to be considered the more holy in proportion as it is more closely connected with the liturgical action . . ." [14] And elsewhere it mentions the singing of the liturgical assembly in one breath with the "actions, gestures and bodily attitudes".[15]

At first sight this might look like a lack of appreciation and diminution of sacred music. In fact, this sentence shows the change in the understanding of singing in the liturgy as part of the liturgical action: singing is no longer understood as "sacred music", a mere embellishment of the liturgical action which could be accomplished more simply and basically just as well with ordinary speech. It is no longer understood as a concession to the solemn celebration of the liturgy as defined by the rubrics but as the natural and human expression of participation in the liturgical celebration.

This concept was adopted and developed by the Instruction *Musicam Sacram*.[16] This is quite clear when we compare the

[13] Art. 3.

[14] Art. 112. This statement seems to be linked with a passage in Pius XII's encyclical *Musicae sacrae disciplina,* which states "that the dignity and effectiveness of Church music are the greater as it comes close to the most holy event in Christian worship, the eucharistic sacrifice of the altar" (II, 5). Cf. the *Const. on the Sacred Liturgy,* Art. 28.

[15] Art. 30.

[16] *Musicam Sacram,* Art. 4b, happens to mention once again the kinds of sacred music and to develop them. We are even given here, for the first time in the history of the Church's legislation on music, a definition of sacred music, and this definition emphasizes the notion of sacred music as repertoire music: "Hence that music, which is composed for the religious service, is called sacred music as it is characterized by holiness and excellence of form" (4a). The reference in a footnote to Pius X is either a misunderstanding or an error. The passage quoted there contains no definition of sacred music, but simply says that sacred music must possess the special qualities of the liturgy at large, namely, holiness and excellence of form. It is significant that this interpolation ignores the conciliar statement on the sacred character of Church music, quoted at the beginning of this section, and goes back to Pius X. In that statement the "sacredness" is defined as "what is not profane". Art. 4a is the only place in the Instruction where the term "polyphony" is still used in a too historical and misunderstood sense. For the rest the text uses the usual terminology: "musica pluribus vocibus", music for several voices. Sections

structure of this Instruction with that of 1958. The latter started
with the forms of liturgical celebration and the various kinds of
sacred music, and then proceeded to lay down how the one
should be made to fit in with the other. *Musicam Sacram,* on
the contrary, begins with the question why there should be singing in the liturgy and then lays down how this singing must
grow out of the nature of the rite and the structure of the
liturgy on the one hand, and on the other, out of the character
and situation of the liturgical assembly. "Particularly those parts
which in themselves demand to be sung, should really be sung,
and this in the way which their nature requires." [17] "In the choice
of Church music for the choir and for the people, the ability of
those that sing should be taken into account. The Church excludes no kind of Church music from her liturgical actions as
long as it corresponds to the spirit of the liturgical action and
the nature of its particular parts and does not obstruct the appropriate active participation by the people." [18] Then the Instruction mentions those that sing in the liturgy,[19] after which it
proceeds to give indications for singing in the liturgy in various
forms of liturgical celebration.[20] Problems concerning particular
kinds of Church music and the musical repertoire are left till the
end.[21] Instead of talking about the embellishment of the solemn
liturgy by means of sacred music, the Instruction states: "The
principal form of the liturgical action is that where the action
takes place with singing." [22] The technical term *in cantu,* up

---

4a and 4b are irrelevant to the Instruction as they are not related to any
other point in the text and hang in mid-air.

[17] Art. 7.

[18] Art. 9.

[19] Art. 13–26.

[20] Singing during Mass, Art. 27–36; singing during the divine office,
Art. 37–41; music during the administration of sacraments or sacra-
mentals, for particular feasts during the Church year, for services of the
"Word", for devotional practices and the religious feast in local Churches,
Art. 42–46.

[21] For the language at services where there is singing and the preservation of the Church's musical heritage, see Art. 47–53. For setting vernacular texts to music, see Art. 54–61. For instrumental music, Art. 62–
67. For Commissions to be set up to foster Church music, Art. 68–69.

[22] Art. 5.

till then reserved for the singing by the priest,[23] is now also applied to the singing of all those that share in the celebration which in the pre-conciliar legislation was designated as "the use of sacred music". In contrast with the view of Church music as "embellishment of the liturgy", it is said "that the true solemnity of a liturgical action does not so much depend on the glamor of the singing and ceremonies", and that "the integrity of the liturgical action, i.e., the appropriate execution of all its parts, must be observed".[24]

The Instruction understands singing in the liturgy no longer as the performance of sacred music or as a matter of adjusting a musical repertoire to the basic factors of the liturgy. It is seen rather as a bodily way in which man expresses himself and communicates with others and as such is part and parcel of the liturgical celebration. In this the Instruction does not disown either the art of music or the musical heritage of the Church. This art has a place in the liturgy. But this art must be part of the liturgy not merely because it is sacred music nor simply because it is tied to a liturgical text. It must "correspond to the spirit of the liturgical action and to the nature of its particular parts". For this all that is required is that it must be "true art", and such "true art" does not spring from a mere following of rules. It presupposes genuine truth, and in matters liturgical this means that it must be a liturgical happening.

Singing as a Liturgical Sign

The Instruction of 1958 distinguished three degrees of participation by the faithful in the solemn Mass: (1) the taking part in the liturgical responses; (2) the singing of the ordinary of the Mass, and first of all, the simpler parts, namely the *Kyrie,* the *Sanctus* and *Benedictus,* and the *Agnus Dei,* while the *Gloria* and *Credo* could be left to the *schola cantorum;* (3) the singing of the proper of the Mass, where all present are sufficiently familiar with plain chant.[25] The varying significance of the sung

[23] Instr. of 1958, Art. 3. Cf. Art. 16–20.
[24] Art. 11.
[25] Art. 25.

parts as ritual acts and part of the liturgical celebration were left out of consideration. The distinction was based on the degree of difficulty in singing plain chant, and the educational standards that were used were wrong. Insofar as singing was concerned, the active participation of the faithful in the liturgical celebration did not suit a participation in the *musica sacra*.

Over against this approach the *Constitution on the Sacred Liturgy* states: "For the liturgy is made up of immutable elements divinely instituted, and of elements subject to change. These not only may but ought to be changed with the passage of time if they have suffered from the intrusion of anything out of harmony with the inner nature of the liturgy or have become unsuited to it. In this restoration, both texts and rites should be drawn up so that they express more clearly the holy things which they signify; the Christian people, so far as possible, should be enabled to understand them with ease and to take part in them fully, actively, and as befits a community." [26] And later on: "In liturgical celebrations each person, minister or layman, who has an office to perform, should do all of, and only, those parts which pertain to his office by the nature of the rite and the principles of the liturgy." [27]

These statements in the Constitution have been understood, particularly at the international congress of the *Consociatio Internationalis Musicae Sacrae,* Milwaukee and Chicago, 1966, to mean that the "sign" and the essence of liturgical singing lay in plain chant. In support, Art. 116 was quoted: "The Church acknowledges Gregorian chant as specially suited to the Roman liturgy; therefore, other things being equal, it should be given pride of place in liturgical functions." The limitation "other things being equal" was ignored, and the conclusion was drawn: "The Gregorian choral performance is an integral part of the Roman liturgy. There may easily be practical difficulties in polyphonic singing as when through an unfortunate choice texts are sung that do not wholly agree with the text of the Roman

[26] Art. 21.
[27] Art. 28.

Missal . . . With singing in the vernacular we are still farther away from the ideal expression of liturgical singing, i.e., the Gregorian choral performance . . . The functions of the individual pieces are levelled down so that singing is then no longer an integral part of the Mass but a constantly changing addition." [28] And so a mangled quotation of the Constitution, out of context, leads us back to the pre-conciliar legislation on "sacred music".

The Instruction *Musicam Sacram* applied the demands of the *Constitution on the Sacred Liturgy* for the true significance and appropriate execution of liturgical actions to singing and drew the consequences for Church music. The text states: "The true shape of a liturgical celebration demands first of all the right distribution and performance of the various tasks . . . It also demands that the function and specific character of each part and each sung piece be taken into proper consideration." [29] That this is not a reference to plain chant as the model is already clear from the fact that the "general directives" of the Instruction nowhere mention plain chant. It is true that the Instruction incorporates Art. 116 of the Constitution about the preeminence of plain chant, "other things being equal". But it does so only where it deals with "liturgical actions that are performed in Latin and accompanied by singing" and states explicitly that this holds only for these liturgical actions.[30]

The nature and function of singing in the liturgical celebration are explicitly defined in the Instruction, at least partly, and it is pointed out that it is here, and not in the model of plain chant, nor in the old assumptions of sacred music, that we must look for the rules which govern the execution and the active participation by the whole liturgical assembly in this singing:

[28] G. Göller, "Strukturprobleme der Missa cantata," in *Musica Sacra*, CVO, 87 (1967, n. 5, p. 136. The report by F. Haberl, "Il quinto congresso internazionale per la musica sacra cattolica," in *Rivista italiana di Musicologia*, vol. II, 1 (1967), pp. 162–73, shows that this essay reproduces a paper read at the Congress.

[29] Art. 6.

[30] Art. 50.

The *Gradual* or responsory after the reading is "by its nature part of the service of the Word. Therefore all should sit and listen, and if possible take part, while it is performed".[31]

"The *Creed,* as an expression of the faith, should be sung as far as possible by all, or at least in such a way as allows the faithful to take an active part in it." [32]

"The *Sanctus,* as an acclamation which concludes the Preface, should be regularly sung by the whole assembly, together with the priest." [33]

The *Agnus Dei,* "to be sung as often as necessary", with the people "joining in at least for the final imprecation", is by the same token defined as a litany, but also as an accompanying chant "since it accompanies the breaking of the bread".[34]

The function of the introit, the offertory and the communion is explained by the Instruction as accompanying the entry or beginning,[35] the preparation of the gifts and the communion of the assembly.[36]

In liturgical singing a difference is therefore made between "singing" and "music".[37] Consequently, the "ordinary" and the "proper" of the Mass are no longer seen as separate entities and can no longer serve as categories when we talk about singing in the liturgy. Hence the Instruction speaks of the "singing of the so-called *Ordinarium Missae*" [38] and regularly uses quotation marks for the term "Ordinarium" and "Proprium Missae". The question is no longer which "ordinary" will be sung or how the "proper" should be performed, but rather how, given the explanations just mentioned and the available musical means,

---

[31] Art. 33.
[32] Art. 34.
[33] Art. 34.
[34] Art. 34.
[35] Art. 36.
[36] Art. 32. Cf. Art. 31.
[37] This was particularly developed at the Freiburg Study Week (see note 3). Another study of this point and of the nature of the various kinds of singing was published by G. Stefani, "L'espressione vocale e musicale nella liturgia," in *Liturgia e cultura* III (Turin, 1967).
[38] Art. 34.

every single rite "can express most clearly the sacred content which it must signify".[39]

Singing as the Expression of the Liturgical Assembly

The Instruction of 1958 carried the following definition: "A Mass is a sung Mass (*Missa in cantu*) when the celebrant really sings those parts which he has to sing according to the rubrics. Otherwise the Mass is a 'read' (low) Mass (*Missa lecta*)." [40] And it specified: "At the sung Mass the celebrant and his ministers as well as the choir and the faithful may only use the Latin language." Only where a centuries-old and immemorial tradition has introduced vernacular singing by the people this may continue on condition that this singing takes place after the liturgical text has been sung in Latin and the habit cannot be prudently abolished. The liturgical words themselves must not be sung in the vernacular.[41] "At the 'read' (low) Mass the celebrant, the altar-server, and the faithful who directly take part in the liturgical action together with the priest, i.e., speak audibly those parts of the Mass which are allotted to them, must in any case use the Latin language. But when, apart from this direct participation, the faithful want to add particular prayers or hymns according to local custom, this may also be done in the vernacular." [42]

The new Instruction *Musicam Sacram* says: "Between the full solemnity of the religious service where all is sung that demands to be sung, and the simplest service where there is no singing at all, there are various intermediate stages according to how much is sung. When choosing the parts to be sung one should begin with the more important, particularly those to be sung by the celebrant or the ministers and answered by the people, and with those that are sung by celebrant and people together; the other parts, which are only sung by the people or the choir, should be added gradually." [43]

[39] *Const. on the Liturgy*, Art. 21.
[40] Art. 3.
[41] Art. 14a.
[42] Art. 14b.
[43] Art. 7.

The meaning of this passage is explained in Articles 29–31 about the celebration of Mass. It applies, of course, also to the other liturgical celebrations, as is pointed out specifically in connection with the celebration of the divine office.[44] That the distinction between *Missa solemnis, cantata* and *lecta,* made in the Instruction of 1958, has been maintained,[45] is in all likelihood due to a juridical concern with stipends. And that in the following sentence the steps from speaking to singing are called "steps in participation according to the abilities of the community", shows that this expression is based on the misunderstanding of that participation by the faithful in the old "sacred music" and those older regulations, quoted above, which the Instruction of 1958 left behind. But this no longer affects the real matter.

The Instruction *Musicam Sacram,* therefore, does not propose rubricist distinctions and rigid plans, but rather tries to provide a framework for singing in the liturgical assembly. It also takes account of the fact that different communities are faced with different situations. Therefore, it states that the celebrant and ministers, with whose singing all singing in the assembly should really begin, at least speak loudly and clearly instead of singing, if they do not have at their disposal the vocal abilities that are required for an appropriate execution of the musical parts; but they should not do this merely for convenience.[46] For the rest, if there are several people available who can perform, the best one should be chosen.[47]

I have already mentioned that "for the choice of Church music for choir and people the ability of the performers should be taken into account".[48] Where possible, there should be a choir, not only in cathedrals and larger churches but also in small churches.[49] Where and when this is not the case a cantor should take the place of the choir.[50] The function of a special precentor

[44] Art. 38.
[45] Art. 28.
[46] Art. 8.
[47] Art. 8.
[48] Art. 9.
[49] Art. 19.
[50] Art. 21.

is only mentioned indirectly, where the Instruction speaks of the singer of the gradual or responsory after the reading.[51]

The choir is part of the community. All restrictions with regard to sex have been dropped,[52] as well as the rubricist perfectionism of the Instruction of 1958 and its misinterpretation of the Motu proprio of Pius X,[53] where it so typically distinguished between choirs that have a liturgical function of their own, or by delegation or none at all.[54] *Musicam Sacram* says that the choir has no particular liturgical function but renders a special liturgical service. "Its task has gained in importance and weight through the regulations of the Council concerning the renewal of the liturgy. It is incumbent on the choir to execute its parts properly according to the various kinds of sung pieces and to encourage the active participation of the faithful in this singing." [55] "According to the various kinds of sung pieces": many pieces are by their nature of an alternating kind, like the *Kyrie* and the *Agnus Dei*. In other cases both tradition and experience have taught us that alternation is particularly useful, as with singing in procession. Again, and for various reasons, alternation is frequently appropriate, perhaps in order to put more life into the singing or to relieve the participation by the people.

The choir's task is, however, by no means limited to this alternation with the people. Whether the choir can sing instead of the whole assembly, or whether it is preferable to let the choir sing and the congregation listen, as at the offertory or the communion, or whether it is better to use instrumental music, as explicitly allowed by Art. 65, for the beginning, the offertory, the communion and the end—all this depends on the nature and character of the particular rite, and on the situation at a particu-

---

[51] Art. 33.
[52] Art. 22.
[53] Cf. *Rinnovamento* etc., p. 101.
[54] Art. 93a, 93c, 99 and 100. This distinction has led to an amusing controversy on whether it is possible in the liturgy to delegate physical abilities, such as the ability to sing. H. Schmitt rejected this in his commentary on the Instruction in *Periodica* 47 (1958), pp. 441f.
[55] Art. 19.

lar liturgical celebration in the case of a particular congregation. One congregation is more fond of singing than another, and even within the same congregation people sing better at one service than at another. The quality and availability of a choir may vary considerably. Thus, the Instruction states: "Particularly when the faithful lack training or polyphony is used, some pieces usually sung by the people may be assigned to the choir, as long as the people are not excluded from other parts that are rightly theirs. But one cannot justify the habit of leaving the whole singing of the 'proper' and the 'ordinary' to a choir and to exclude the people from all participation in the singing." [56] It is to be noted that the Instruction does not count the *Sanctus* as a "song" but as an acclamation,[57] and that it does not speak of the "Credo" but of the "confession of faith" so that it should not be mistaken for a kind of hymn in the proper sense of the word.[58]

It is true that Art. 4b of *Musicam Sacram,* like the pre-conciliar ordinances about sacred music, only counts choral pieces, and not solos, as Church music.[59] But elsewhere it says

[56] Art. 16c. Cf. Art. 34.

[57] Art. 34. Cf. Art. 16a and 29.

[58] Art. 34. Cf. Art. 30b.

[59] In spite of this one commentator, who prided himself in knowing about an "earlier draft" of the Instruction, he managed to read the following into the text: "The things people were saying: Credo and Sanctus must never be sung in a way which would exclude the people; and even that it was wrong to divide the Credo between choir and people since the Credo is the confession of faith of the whole congregation! How many of our faithful have enough stamina to sing right through a Credo? But here the identification of *actuosus* and *activus* is turned into a principle. Such exaggerations are no longer possible. It is hardly necessary to stress once again: the people's participation in the Sanctus, also in the Latin Mass, is our primary concern and is easy to achieve; but on the basis of what structural law is it required that this can never be otherwise?" (Karl Günter Peusquens, "Kleiner Kommentar zur Instructio de musica in sacra liturgia," in *Pastoralblatt für die Diözesen Aachen, Berlin, Essen und Köln* 19 (1967), p. 173. The Instruction avoids the style of pre-conciliar regulations and says that "the Sanctus, as the concluding acclamation of the Preface, should as a rule be sung by the whole congregation together with the priest" (Art. 34). It does not say: "It is strictly forbidden to have the Sanctus sung by the choir." And from this the author draws the conclusion that the Instruction condemns as an exaggeration anyone who takes it seriously, and that it adopts the view of those who understand singing in the liturgy

explicitly that "music for one or more voices, whether from the traditional heritage or modern compositions, must be respected, encouraged and on suitable occasions used".[60] With the proviso that the competent local authority should decide "whether particular, traditional vernacular texts, linked with musical compositions, may be used, even when they do not exactly correspond to officially approved translations of liturgical texts",[61] it is clear that our liturgy stands open, not only to the Catholic context, musical heritage and modern compositions but also to texts that have become traditional in separated Churches. This applies to compositions for choirs and solos as well as for congregational singing.

Finally, the appropriate authority can allow "the substitution of the sung pieces gathered in the *Graduale Romanum* for introit, offertory and communion by others" where this is done by legitimate usage as long as these pieces correspond to "the respective parts of the Mass, the feast or the liturgical season" and the texts are approved by local authority.[62] This concerns not

---

not as a participation in the liturgy but as a taking part in the execution of sacred music. Only by confusing the issue like this can one conclude that the principle of active participation leads to meaningless activism and a rejection of Church music as an art. The art of music has obviously a place in the liturgy: the renewal of the liturgy simply offers it wholly new tasks and opportunities. But, precisely as genuine art, Church music must take note of the kind of rite and of what it must signify. It is therefore the more sacred and the more truly artistic the more directly it springs from the rite itself. Both the artistic and the liturgical aspects of Church music are neither rejected in principle nor glibly passed by when the demand for active participation is contrasted with the idea of a "liturgical listening to music": "It remains part of human self-realization to be always ready to listen. How perilous is the condition of a man who can no longer listen. His knowledge of truth is limited, in matters of justice he is narrow, and love will certainly suffer. Who can forget the Lord's exhortation: Let him who has ears to hear with, hear. The *actuosa participatio* also implies a live ability to listen. We often say that all prayer is ultimately a listening to the will of God. Let us make room for such listening in our religious services. I think I may say that we are badly in need of a little more listening piety" ("Liturgie und Kirchenmusik im Sinne der Konstitution des zweiten vatikanischen Konzils über die hl. Liturgie," by Johannes Overath, in *Musica Sacra* CVO 84 (1964, n. 7/8, p. 194).

[60] Art. 50c.
[61] Art. 55.

only the hymn, but also the choir, the cantor and, above all, the composer. The musical form is already for a large part pre-determined by the *Graduale Romanum*. The very distance between the contemporary composer and the musical texts of Gregorian plain chant makes him often look on this plain chant as the classic model: this prevents him from seeing that he only should concern himself with the singing of a liturgical celebration, at the beginning, the offertory and at communion.[63] Ultimately, however, the significance of this statement lies in the fact that it makes the local Church responsible for the choice of its liturgical singing and that it allows the local Church to create its own liturgy for its own liturgical gathering.

And what about Latin? For *Musicam Sacram* the liturgical language is not a problem concerning its "general directives". It is mentioned later on when it has finished with singing in the various kinds of liturgical celebration and in connection with the "preservation of the treasure of Church music": "According to the *Constitution on the Sacred Liturgy* the use of the Latin language will be maintained in the Latin rites insofar as this does not conflict with special privileges." To this, the Instruction adds that "the abilities of the actual community" must be taken into consideration.[64]

[62] Art. 32. Cf. Art. 36 and 65: "At the beginning, before the priest enters, at the offertory, the communion and at the end of the Mass instrumental music can be played.

[63] Cf. the reply given by a noted composer, Max Baumann, to an invitation by the Allgemeine Caecilien-Verband, to set to music the texts of the Proper of the Mass in German translation: "Plain chant is so unique to me and such a rich source from every point of view that I would consider it presumptuous to replace it by any work of my own. Compared with the organically developed forms of plain chant, created in the anonymity and profound religious faith of that age, any short-sighted replacement can only be makeshift. Confronted with this supremely noble heritage of centuries of well-molded forms and formulas, any 'creative imitator' is in a hopeless situation. Our contemporary creative music, with its harmonic tensions, cannot touch that simple monody. It can only be expressed in the language of our time" (*Musica Sacra* CVO 84, 1964, n. 7/8, p. 214). That would mean that it is no longer possible today to compose liturgical music, because the musical language of today differs from that of plain chant!

[64] Art. 47.

PART III
DOCUMENTATION
CONCILIUM

Office of the Executive Secretary
Nijmegen, Netherlands

Concilium General Secretarial/*Nijmegen, Netherlands*

Non-Christian Burial Rites

INTRODUCTION

Even a superficial glance at a standard work on burial rites such as *Funeral Customs the World Over* shows that a documentation, such as this section wishes to provide, can obviously not pretend to any kind of completeness. Nor is this really necessary in this liturgical volume where we are looking for ways of renewing the rite of burial. It is, however, important to see how relative are certain parts of our present Christian rite. A comparison with rites and customs of other religions soon shows that certain parts of this Christian funeral rite are more closely connected with popular traditions, particular notions about hygiene, a universally human respect for the dead and the sense of impotence, of inability to prolong the life of a loved one, rather than with the Christian belief in a risen life. When we wish to adjust the present funeral rite, we shall then take a more detached view of certain parts of this rite and perhaps find valuable elements in other religions which might be integrated as variations into a more supple basic rite.

We deliberately have also included in this documentation the attitude of the Marxist and of the modern American citizen. These two clearly show that the burial rite is seen from an angle which is totally different from that of the traditional great religions. This is quite obvious in "mortuary science". Here the main concern is to make man's death also profitable for the businessman. When one realizes that the American spends twice as much on his burial than on medical care for his present life, one realizes also that this systematic exploitation of man's grief has not been economically unsuccessful. Yet, even this angle of "care for the dead" can provide valuable information about the kind of background from which modern man can be approached.

In order to make this information as objective as possible and to see what happens in the various groups at a burial, we have put four questions to qualified representatives of these groups: 1. What happens when your group wants to pay its last respects to a dead person? 2. Do you use various rites which allow for a certain improvisation, or is your rite a closed and static procedure? 3. Does the way in which you show respect for the dead at burial correspond to specific ideas about death or a possible afterlife? 4. Does your group show a tendency to come to some renewal of the existing funeral rite? The answer to these questions is the real point of the following documentation.

DEATH AND BURIAL IN AFRICA

Jacobus Theuws, O.F.M. Lubumbashi, Congo

The very variety of rites which accompany an African burial proves that every death affects the community as a whole. It also proves that for the African death is not the end of man. The way in which the body is treated depends of course on the idea the group has about the manner in which the "soul" continues to exist, and therefore on the nature and composition of a human being, the existence of "world of the dead", and so on. It should be noted, *en passant,* that this rather vague notion of an afterlife does not imply immortality.

The manner of burying depends also on the social position,

the sex, the age of the defunct person—in short, on the whole cultural context. Although all kinds of burials occur, some of which only apply to exceptional cases or abnormal persons, the most common is that of inhumation. When a body is wholly destroyed, the idea is to deprive the dead person of any material support which might allow him to protract his presence among the living.

Apart from the rites with which the seriously ill brother is surrounded in order to defend his life with the strength of the community gathered around him, the words and gestures that accompany the burial suggest a twofold attitude. The community is concerned about itself: death has contaminated all things and all members. Life has stopped. Part of it has died and the whole is overshadowed by the situation of death. If the head of the village has died, the whole village is doomed: fires are extinguished, work ceases, the fields are neglected or even laid waste, cattle are slaughtered or simply destroyed. At the burial or at the end of the mourning period, life must be set going again with the help of ritual purification, noisy rites, funeral meals, various contests and so forth. There was danger of losing touch with the life of the cosmos, and now it must be caught up with again. The stricken community must occupy its place again in the greater society. Death ostracized a part of the community and the "others" withdrew. The ban is lifted again by means of reintegration rites, the putting off of mourning and the destruction of the symbols of death.

Another source of anxiety is the fate of the dead person. There, too, one can broadly distinguish between rites of separation and rites of integration. The dead person leaves the community only with great reluctance. With the use of gentle force, ruse and sometimes frightening violence, one tries to keep him out of home and village. The body is taken out through a hole in the wall, he is taken to the grave by a roundabout way, the house is purified or destroyed, the feet of the body are bound together, the members of the body are broken, it is pegged to the ground, a fire is lit on the way back, and so on. All this is in order to prevent the dead person from returning to his home. He must not only move to the land of the ancestors, but must be accepted and be given his place there. For him it is a "passage through", and the living are responsible for the success of this journey. Depending on the notions about afterlife and the position and career of the dead person, he is provided with money for the journey, put into his hand or mouth, as well as with his weapons, tools and the symbols of his rank and dignity. Sometimes he is provided even with some of his cattle, his slaves and wives: the "shadow" or "soul" of things, animals and human beings accompany the life-shadow of the defunct to the twilight of the far-distant underworld, a world of bleak shadows. The dead person is told: we are not guilty of your death; we do not know who killed you; take the killer with you; do not send us evil dreams, etc. Sometimes these last words, which may be spoken by the eldest son, become a kind of ritual abuse: go away, so that I can take your place. As in other such rites the dead person reaches his new situation only gradually: the body "resists" while it is taken to the grave and is sometimes buried two or three times.

Yet, however anxious the people are to eliminate the dead person he must remain in contact with the living. He takes his place with his ancestors and becomes a "spirit", a tutelary spirit. Certain events, interpreted as signs, show the disposition and the will of the dead person. He asks for a little "fire to warm himself"; he demands a cult. The continuity of his existence depends on his being remembered by the living. This existence would cease if he were forgotten. His name therefore lives on in the names of the children. Should he, however, return in order to torment, then his body is burned or poison is poured into his mouth.

The attitude of both the living and the dead is therefore always marked by a certain ambiguity. We find this basic pattern again in the choice of burial sites. The body may be left unburied and the house abandoned, leaving the body more or less as a worthless thing to wild animals, or, particularly in the case of a great and powerful personage, the dead person may be buried in his own hut or kraal. Elsewhere only the skull or some other part of the body is kept. Between these extremes there runs a whole gamut of variations. Today, especially in more modern places, some hair or nails are taken from the body to be interred in ancestral ground so that the spirit may come to rest. The shadow of life, which left the body at death, clings as long as possible to some bodily element. It is enough to eliminate, to bury, or to honor this more or less symbolic element to get into touch with the dead person.

Finally, it must be repeated that all this is only given its true meaning when seen in the whole context of a concrete and living culture.

Chief Elements in the Mohammedan Burial Rite

Albert Nader, Beirut, Lebanon

This brief study is restricted to the Moslems of the four Sunnite rites, each of which will be indicated by initials: Shafi'ites (S); Hanbalites (HB); Hanifites (H); Malikites (M), and to Imamite Shi'ites (I). Where there is agreement between the four Sunnite rites and the Shi'ites I shall describe them as (Unanimous).

1. The Position of the Body

The dead man's face must be turned to face Qibla (Mecca). The body must be laid on its back, the soles of the feet turned toward Qibla in such a way that if it were held in a sitting position it would be facing away from Qibla (S, L), or laid on its right side, with the face turned toward Qibla; it must also have this position in the tomb (HB, H, M).

2. *Washing the Body*

a. The object of washing is to purify the dead man before burying him, for he must present himself to God with a spotless body. However, anyone who has died a martyr's death in battle with an infidel is not washed, for he is already purified by blood (Unanimous). As for an aborted child, it is only washed if it miscarries at four months or later (HB, I), or if it resembles a human being (H), or if it is of an age at which it could have lived (M), or if it miscarries after the sixth month, or has only died after birth, or if it has a fully human body (S). As for the dead man whose body is missing any parts, he will be washed if the larger part of the body remains, or half the body including the head (H), or if there is at least two-thirds of the body (M), or if there is only a little of it left (HB, S), or if the breast remains, or the part containing the heart, or any part with bone in it (I).

b. The person who does the washing should, if possible, be of the same sex. However, a surviving spouse may wash his or her dead partner (all except H). For (H) a husband cannot wash his dead wife, because death has ended his marital rights over her, but the wife may wash her dead husband, for she must remain a widow for a set period during which she cannot remarry; during that time she remains dependent on her dead husband; if she should become pregnant during that period, the children will be those of her dead husband (H). If the dead man had repudiated his wife—whether permanently or temporarily—she cannot wash him (S, M); if the repudiation was only temporary, then she can (I). A woman can wash the body of a dead boy less than three years old, and a man that of a dead girl less than three years old (I); this is possible if the child is less than four (H) or less than seven (HB), or if the dead boy is under eight and the girl less than two years and eight months (M).

c. As to the method of washing the body, it will be washed three times: first with water mixed with a little milk, then with water mixed with camphor, and lastly with pure, clear water;

each time one begins by washing the head, then the right side, and lastly the left side (I). In the four Sunnite rites one need only wash the body once with pure, clear water, and in no special order. The body is washed with cool water (S, HB, M, I) or with warm water (H). When there is no water available, they perform the "tayamum", in which dust from the ground is used instead of water; this is also done when there is a risk that water will harm a body badly damaged by grave illness; the body must be kept looking as much like itself as possible before being buried.

3. *Embalming the Body*

One rubs with camphor the seven parts of the body used when prostrating oneself for prayer: the forehead, the two hands, the two knees and the ends of the two big toes. This order is followed by (I) who also embalm the nose, but not by the four Sunnite rites.

4. *The Shroud*

The body must be wrapped in a shroud (Unanimous). That shroud must include a single piece of material in which the whole body is wrapped (the four Sunnite rites), but they recommend that there be three pieces altogether. For (I) these three pieces are obligatory: one to wrap the body from the navel to the knees, another from the shoulders to the knees, and the third for the whole body (I). The shroud must not be of silk, nor embroidered with gold thread: rich and poor are equal in death.

5. *The Burial Prayer*

a. This is efficacious only after the body has been prepared for burial. There is no funeral prayer for martyrs (S, HB, M), though with (H, I) there is. It may be said for abortions from the fourth month on (HB, H), or only for newborn children who give some sign of life before they die (S, M); with (I) it is said only for children who die when more than six years of age.

b. Who says the prayer? For (I) the washing and prayer for the burial are efficacious only when performed by the person whose duty they are—that is, the person closest in succession to the dead man; however someone else can be delegated to perform the task instead. The four Sunnite rites say nothing about who is to perform the preparation of the body, but the prayer must be said by the person chosen by the dead man beforehand, or by the closest in succession, or by a local dignitary.

c. How is the prayer said? The person who says it, having turned to face Qibla, stands at the bedside on the right hand side of the litter on which the body lies on its back. First, he expresses his intention to pray. This formula varies from one rite to another.

Malikites: "Allah is most great. O God, forgive the sins of this dead man.—Allah is most great. O God, have mercy upon him and upon us.—Allah is most great. O God, forgive him, and forgive us our sins.—Allah is most great. O God, may he dwell in thy vast paradise.—Salvation be with you all."

Hanafites: "Allah is most great. God be praised; let us give thanks to God.—Allah is most great. O God, bless Mohammed. —Allah is most great. O God, have mercy on this dead man.— Allah is most great. Salvation be with you; the mercy of God be with you all" (this final invocation is said twice).

Shafi'ites and Hanbalites: "Allah is most great. (Then follows the Fatiha, the first chapter of the *Koran.*)—Allah is most great. O God, bless Mohammed.—Allah is most great. O God, have mercy upon him and upon us. Allah is most great. Salvation be with you."

Shi'ites: "Allah is most great. I declare that there is no God but Allah, and Mohammed is his prophet.—Allah is most great. O God, bless Mohammed and his family.—Allah is most great. O God, forgive the sins of all men and women who believe.— Allah is most great. O God, forgive the sins of this dead man (if the body is of a child: O God, forgive the sins of his parents). —Allah is most great."

d. Where is the prayer said? It should preferably be said at the mosque (S); it may be said at the mosque if there is no danger of desecrating it (HB, I); for (H) however, it is un- thinkable for it to be said at the mosque.

e. When is the burial prayer said? It can be said at any time (S, I); it cannot be said either at sunrise or at sunset (HB, H, M).

6. *The Funeral Procession*

The litter, covered with a soft carpet and carried shoulder- high, goes ahead of the mourners who continually repeat: "There is no God but Allah; Mohammed is Allah's prophet." Nowadays, given the distances between the cemeteries and people's homes, the litter is placed in a special car, and the procession follows in cars or even on motorcycles (this happens at Rabat, in Morocco, for instance).

7. *The Burial*

The body must be put in a tomb hollowed out of the earth; it must be laid on its right side with its face turned toward Qibla. A husband will bury his dead wife; failing that, it will be done by one of her *maharim*—those permitted to see her face during her lifetime, or it will be a woman, or someone honorable (I, S, M); but for (HB, H) the husband cannot bury his dead wife, for death has broken all the bonds between them. Whoever goes down into the tomb to place the body in it must go with bare head and feet, and must unfasten his clothes and say: "In the name of Allah. By the religion of Allah's prophet. O God, may his tomb be wide. May this dead man rejoin his prophet. O God, if he has done good, increase that good; if he has done ill, forgive him, have mercy on him and pardon his sins." It is also recommended that the "Fatiha" be read.

The Shi'ites, in Iraq and Iran especially, prefer to be buried at Najaf or Karbala (in southern Iraq), near the tomb of 'Ali (the prophet's son-in-law), or of 'Ali's son, Hosayn.

The tomb must not be above ground level (S, I), for it is an established fact that the prophet made the tomb of his son

Ibrahim at ground level. However, (H, HB and M) prefer to make the tomb vaulted in shape, since to them a flat shape has become symbolic for certain non-Moslem peoples. An inscription carved upon marble will give the dead man's name, the date of his death, and a verse from the *Koran*.

———◆◀◆▶◆———

Muslim Burial

Qudratullah Hafiz, Den Haag, Netherlands

For Islam life after death is part of this life. All that man does, says or thinks in this life is preserved. In afterlife everything is again made visible for the believer.[1] At the death of a Muslim, man or woman, old or young, a service is held in the presence of the mortal remains. This service is called *Salât-al-djanâ'is*. *Djanâ'is* is the plural of Djinâza, "the dead body on the bier" or "the bier".[2]

When someone has died the body is washed with soap or some other disinfectant. First those parts are washed that are usually washed at a ritual washing (Wudu). Then the whole body is cleaned,[3] after which it is swathed in one or more white cloths (Bu 23, 19, 20, 27) and scents are used (Bu 23, 21). If the dead person is a martyr or has fallen in battle, the body is neither washed nor clothed (Bu 23, 73).

As a token of reverence the body is then carried on the shoulders to the burial site, either on a bier or, if necessary, in a coffin. The body may, however, be carried by other means.

When the bier of a Jew passed the Prophet, he stood up to honor the dead person, and he commanded the Muslim to do the same (Bu 23, 50).

To take part in the service is called *Fard Kifaya*. "It is enough

[1] The *Quran*, the holy book of Islam; 28, 78; 29, 65; 18, 103, 107; 7, 33; 45, 25–30; 50, 3–7; 75, 4–16.
[2] E. W. Lane, *Arabic-English Lexicon*.
[3] Al-Hafiz Abū 'Abd-Allah Muhammed Ibn Isma'il Al-Buchari, *As-Sahih al-Buchari* (Bu) 23, 8. 9. 11.

if a few Muslims take part in the service." This service can be held anywhere. All who take part must perform the Wudu. The bier is put down in front, and the Imân stands with his face turned toward the middle of the bier (Bu 23, 64). The people stand in rows, according to the number present, and face toward the *Qibla* (Mecca). The service begins with a *Takbir;* as it is spoken, hands are raised to the height of the ears and then, as in prayer, folded on the chest. During the service there are four such *Takbirs,* during the recitation of which people remain standing (Bu 23, 65). After the first *Takbir,* a *Dhikr* or *Sanâ* is said, together with an *Al-Fâtiha;* the second is followed by a *Salawât-annabi* and the third by a special prayer. With the exception of the *Takbirs* these prayers must be said in a low voice.[4] The fourth *Takbir* is followed by the *Taslim* during which the head turns from right to left.

When the service is over, the body is taken away and buried with the prayer: "In the name of Allah, and with Allah, and as the messenger of Allah" (Tr 8, 53). The grave is dug in such a way that the body can be placed with its face toward Mecca. It is usually four to six feet deep, and the side is hollowed out to make room for the body. This hollowing-out is called *Ladh* and is not required if a coffin is used for the burial. The grave is then closed and again a prayer for the dead is recited. After this all go home.[5]

The rite for a child only differs from that of the adult in that the prayer after the third *Takbir* is changed. The burial service for children does not require a prayer for forgiveness. It is replaced by a petition that the dead child may obtain forgiveness and recompense for the parents.

Up to this time the Muslims show no tendency to effect any changes in the existing rite.

[4] Al Iman Al-Hafiz Abü Isa Mohammed Ibn Isâ, *Al-Djami' al Tirmidhi* (Tr) 8, 37. Sjaich Wali al-Den Muhammed Ibn 'Abd-Allah, *Al-Misjkât al-Masâbih* 5, 5–11.

[5] Abü Dawüd, *Sunnah* 20, 67. Cf. M. M. Ali, *The Religion of Islam*; Ahmadiyya Moslim Missie, *Gebedboek van de Moslims.*

The Funeral Rites of the Hindus

Cyril Papali, O.C.D. Rome, Italy

Hinduism is exceptionally rich in ritual, and the rites of the funeral are perhaps the most interesting ones after those of the marriage. They were codified during the two or three centuries immediately preceding the Christian era, but the rites themselves are much older. As Hinduism is spread over a vast subcontinent and divided into innumerable sects, ceremonies differ from place to place in minor details, but the essential rites are faithfully observed by orthodox Hindus everywhere. We give below a short description of the most common rites.

When a sick person, of whatever caste or sex, is about to die, the last sacrament, *antyeṣṭi,* is administered to him. The priest approaches the deathbed carrying in his hand a potion called *pancagavyam* (the five products of the cow), and with prayers from the scriptures administers it to the dying person who drinks it, reciting: "I receive this sacrament of *pancagavyam* in expiation of all my sins knowingly or unknowingly committed."

As the moment of death draws near, the patient is laid on the ground, it being a most desirable thing to die in the arms of mother earth. Immediately after the death a lighted lamp is placed at the head of the corpse and preparations made for the funeral. The eldest son of the deceased is to officiate in the ceremony or, in the absence of sons, the nearest male relation.

In Vedic times burial was the most common mode of disposing of the dead, but by the 4th or 3rd century B.C. it had been already superseded by cremation as the only legitimate form of funeral. Manu, the great law-giver, makes an exception in the case of infants: "If an infant under two years old should die, let the body be adorned with flowers and carried to a clean place and buried; the bones shall not be collected afterward" (Laws of Manu V, 68). The same is the rule for ascetics who have made the vow of total renunciation: they are buried like infants as they have nothing to expiate. The concession of Manu in favor of infants is sometimes given a liberal interpretation so as to include young boys before their "initiation" ceremony and girls before their marriage. Those who die of contagious diseases are also buried without delay. For the rest, most of the Hindus cremate their dead.

After the body has been washed and clothed, the karma-karta (officiating person) immolates clarified butter, rice, etc., in the sacred fire, reciting suitable prayers—for example: "O Agni, look down on me; grant me thy benevolence and favor; with thy seven tongues lick up this holocaust of mine." Then the body is laid on the bier and the procession formed—all in single file behind the bier, elders first, juniors following, men and women in separate groups. At the head of the procession walks the chief mourner, the karma-karta, carrying in his hand the sacred fire. If the means of the family permit, some animal is also led along for sacrifice. No band or musical instruments accompany a cremation procession; they may be hired for a burial procession. A curious ceremony takes place three times on the way: the procession is stopped, the face of the deceased uncovered and a formula repeated over it: *OM jīva, punarāgacchasi va?* (O soul, hast thou returned?). This is the official confirmation of death.

Meanwhile, in the cremation ground a shallow excavation in the form of a grave is made to receive the funeral pyre: this is a relic of the ancient custom of burying the dead. After the procession has reached the place, the karma-karta blesses the excavated spot, sprinkling water on it with a branch of the çāmi tree, reciting the following verses from the Veda: "Depart [ye evil spirits], slink away from here; the Fathers have made for him this place of rest, distinguished by days and waters and bright lights" (RigVeda X, 14, 9). Then the funeral pyre is arranged with logs of wood (sandalwood if the family is rich enough to afford it) and the corpse laid naked on it: one must leave the world naked as one entered it. With many more ceremonies the sacred fire is applied to the logs while select verses from the RigVeda are repeated. Some of the most interesting specimens are given below.

"Open thy arms, O earth; receive the dead with gentle pressure and with loving welcome. Enshroud him tenderly, even as a mother folds her soft vestment round the child she loves".

(*Ibid*. X, 18, 11)

Evidently this refers to the ancient custom of burying the dead.

"Soul of the dead! Depart, take thou the path—the ancient path—by which our ancestors have gone before thee; thou shalt look upon the two kings, mighty Varuna and Yama, delighting in oblations; thou shalt meet the Fathers and receive the recompense of all thy stored-up offerings above. Leave thou thy sin and imperfections here; return unto thy home once more; assume a glorious form. . . .

Advance to meet the Fathers who, with hearts kindly disposed toward thee, dwell in bliss with Yama; and do thou, O mighty god, entrust him to thy guards to bring him to thee, and grant him health and happiness eternal"

(*Ibid*. X, 14, 7–11)

When the body has been reduced to ashes, the karma-karta repeats the following:

"We living men, survivors, now return and leave the dead. May our oblations please the gods and bring us blessings! Now we go to dance and jest and hope for longer life"

(*Ibid*. X, 18, 3)

However, the mourning is not over yet. All bathe themselves, change their dress and wait for the stars to appear before they return home. They have all been fasting from the moment the death occurred, but this night nothing can be cooked. So they partake of whatever edible may be found in the house and for three days abstain from salt.

Special services for the departed soul are held for ten days. Meanwhile the bones are collected in an earthen urn and buried in a suitable place to the accompaniment of other rites. But those who can afford it take the remains to Benares to be deposited in the sacred river Ganges, for "as long as the bones of a man lie in the Ganges, so long shall he be honored in heaven", says the old proverb.

But the dead are not easily forgotten. The "occasional rites" for the dead, one on the eighth day of every month and another on the anniversary of the death, are continued for three generations. Even when they cease, there is the general libation for all the dead ancestors which is a perpetual daily act of religion in every Hindu household.

Chinese Confucianism and Burial

Louis Wei Tsing-sing, Paris, France

In China, there is no State religion, but only a popular religion based on Confucianism, Buddhism and Taoism. These three, at once religious and moral, are three forms which together in effect make up a single mystical body and a perfect ecumenism. In Chinese they say "San-kiao-y-kia", which means that the three religions are one family.

Confucius commanded his disciples to serve their parents in their lifetime with loving care, and after death with mourning, offerings and a solemn burial.[1] Confucius' doctrine is one of moral, political and social philosophy similar to that of his great contemporaries, Socrates, Plato and Aristotle.

Therefore, when a Confucianist man of letters dies, his family invites Buddhist bonzes and Taoist priests to perform the re-

[1] *Le Hiao-king,* sacred book of filial piety, published in French in Paris, 1889, Chapter I.

ligious service in the same brightly-lit chapel and to walk in the same cortege at the funeral. The actual ceremonies will vary according to area, local tradition, custom, social class, and so on, but the inspiration that underlies them is always the same, actuated by religious feeling and by respect and gratitude toward the dead. In the past, religious funerals took place almost everywhere in China, just as in the West almost all the baptized, even if they have not practiced their religion, are buried with a church service because it is the custom.

Confucius, who was a religious man, though not in the strict sense, did not believe in the immortality of the soul; however he did not deny the existence of soul or spirit, and he did honor the dead. "One should give offerings to the dead," he used to say, "as though their spirits were present." [2]

It is, of course, well known that ancestor-worship which is so dear to the hearts of the Chinese, and indeed all expressions of honor for the dead, were condemned by Benedict XIV in 1742, during the course of the so-called Chinese rite disputes. This made a painful and complete break between the unfortunate Christians and the whole of the non-Christian population, both in their family relationships and the wider social context.

In 1929, China observed national mourning for Dr. Sun Yat-sen, a practicing Protestant who was the founder and father of the Chinese people's revolution. Msgr. Celso Costantini, then the apostolic delegate in Peking, was officially invited to take part in the solemn ceremonies. He accepted on condition that the Chinese define the nature of those ceremonies. This is the statement made by the Chinese government: "We cannot use any superstitious rites at the funeral, because Dr. Sun Yat-sen was a Christian; but neither can we have a Christian funeral, because China is pagan." Msgr. Costantini, like the leaders of the other diplomatic missions, bowed his head three times before Dr. Sun Yat-sen's body. [3]

[2] Confucius, *Conversations* (Liun-lu), Book III, 12.
[3] Costantini, Celso, *Con i missionari in Cina* II (Rome, 1946), pp. 105–09.

Burial rites still take place under the present regime. As in Europe, everyone still pays solemn final homage to statesmen, national heroes, great patriots, outstanding scholars, and so on. There are a few moments of reverent silence before the body— or the portrait—of the dead man; crowns and flowers are offered, but no candles; funeral speeches are made.

Party leaders often prefer cremation. In all the large towns in China there are crematoria, though the mass of the people still think cremation is an act of profanation, for to them the dead body is a sacred object; that is why ordinary people, and especially country people, punctiliously observe all the old burial rites.

We may quote an example from 1964, when an active Communist from northern China died, and his family prepared chickens, wine, and sticks of incense to offer his dead spirit. The party leaders then summoned the members of the family to explain to them that there was no spirit, no soul there, and that to perform such superstitious practices at the funeral would give everyone a very bad impression.

Again, an old man of 77 one day said to his son, who was an active Communist: "I am old, and the other world is drawing near. How much money can you spend on me [for funeral expenses]?" The son replied: "We are living in a new world, and all our traditions have changed." To this the poor old man could only say: "The new funerals are good, but no one in our village has them yet, and how can I be the only exception?" [4]

The *People's Daily* of Peking, in its editorial of April 25, 1964, declared that the old rituals must be done away with, but tactfully, for such traditions have deep roots which cannot easily be destroyed, and above all, one must study the reactions of the people.

To sum up, even today most of the Chinese people continue to bury their dead more or less religiously, depending on what is possible in the existing situation, and their doing so is tolerated by the authorities.

[4] Quoted from *China News Analysis,* Hong Kong, May 8, 1964, p. 7.

Every year, on the feast of the Tsing-ming—the Chinese All Saints'—in March or April, nearly all the members of the family will go to the cemetery and put the graves of their dead in order with the utmost reverence. Public opinion considers this to be a personal matter, bearing only upon human feeling and affection.

It is often asked why it is permitted to put crowns and flowers on the graves whereas it is forbidden to burn bank notes. This is the answer given by the Communist press: "The difference between offering flowers and burning bank notes is great. To offer flowers is a sign of commemoration, a mark of respect and remembrance, but to burn bank notes is completely superstitious; it indicates a belief that there is a soul or a spirit there who still needs money in the other world." [5]

In short, Chinese Christians must give the most serious thought to these great upheavals that are going on in regard to burial, in the light of their own religious and human awareness. One may nonetheless wonder whether it is true that a general reform in Christian funeral liturgy is absolutely necessary and urgent in the context of the life of the nation.

A Sketch of the Buddhist Funeral

Jan Yün-Hua, Santiniketan, W. Bengal, India

Considering the long historical traditions, extensive geographical factors, numerous population and divergent backgrounds of the countries where Buddhism spread, it is impossible to give an accurate account on the topic within such a limited space. Neither is it possible to explain and analyze how the rite was performed or its significance. The present paper is only a short sketch on

[5] *People's Daily*, Peking, April 10, 1964, p. 2.

the main features of Buddhist funeral ceremonies; unusual or minor cases have not been discussed.

Unlike other religions of the world, there were no rigid rules of funeral rites in early Buddhist scriptures, nor does any uniform regulation exist in the Buddhist community. This is probably due to the teachings of Buddha. According to Buddhist doctrines, all transient beings, including mankind, are component. When the condition is suitable, they would be composed, and when it changes, they are decomposed. Therefore, birth is a thing which is not worthy of celebration, and death is nothing important. Both of them are only parts of the chain of nature. Buddhism is a philosophy which helps its followers to understand impermanence as the true nature of the transient world. There is nothing that one can grasp about it; they must see the nature of things and free themselves from the chain of birth and death. Moreover, Gautama Buddha himself denied all usefulness of any ritualistic forms, nor did he rely on God or Karma. These basic teachings made Buddhists give no importance to the rite of death.

According to a Book of Disciplines belonging to the Sarvastivadin school of Buddhism, when Buddha was alive, some monks pleaded with him to give instructions about the disposal of dead monks. Buddha ruled that the corpse should be cremated. However, if necessary firewood is not available, the corpse may be thrown into a river, or buried, or put inside a forest.[1] This clearly indicates the flexible attitude of Buddhists toward the funeral.

Since Buddha was cremated after his Great Departure, cremation became a more widely accepted way of funeral in the Buddhist world. In India, when a monk passes away, and after one has examined and declared that he is dead, the corpse is sent on a bier to a cremation ground and burned there in the same day. Under the light of burning flame, friends of the deceased sit by the side of the ground. A skillful man is appointed to recite one

---

[1] *Taishu shinshu daizokyo*, ed. J. Takakusu *et al.*, n. 1451 (Tokyo, 1924–29), pp. 286f.

or two pages from the *Anitya-sutra,* the *Scripture on Impermanence.* The friends return to their monastery when the corpse
is consumed by fire. Before entering into their monasteries, they
have to bathe with their clothes on, and then change to dry
clothes and go back to their own apartments, cleanse the ground
of the room with cow-dung powders, and then meditate on the
impermanent nature of beings.[2] To a large extent, this simple
procedure has been followed by the Buddhists of other countries
too, though there are certain variations and modifications. In
Ceylon, when a person of high rank dies, his body is usually
burned with ceremony. The body is first laid out, and then washed
by pouring pitchers of water, covered with a linen cloth and carried forth to burn. After reaching the place of cremation, the
body is placed upon a pile of wood some two to three feet high;
more wood is then added upon the corpse, the top is covered
with some kind of a canopy, and the dead person set afire. After
all is burned, the mourners sweep together the ashes into the
manner of a sugar-loaf, hedge the place, and sow herbs there.
People of inferior quality are interred in some convenient place
in the woods, carried there by two or three of their friends and
buried without ceremony. They place the body on its back, head
to the West and feet to the East. After the burial has been done,
the friends wash themselves.[3]

In the Indo-China Peninsula, soon after a man dies, his relations wash the corpse, shave the head, and place it on a bedstead
covered with a white cloth. A white canopy is erected over the
bedstead and lamps are lit by the side of his head and feet. A
coffin is made and the body is put into it; scented water is sprin-
kled, and there is loud wailing by the women relatives. The coffin is carried to the grave, accompanied by musicians and Buddhist mendicants. After the arrival, the coffin is carried around
the grave three times, and a roll of white cloth is placed on one

[2] Cf. I-Tsing, *A Record of the Buddhist Religion as Practised in India
and the Malay Archipelago,* tr. J. Takakusu (Oxford, 1896), pp. 81–82.
[3] T. W. Rhys Davids, tr., *Buddhist Suttas, Sacred Book East* (Oxford,
1881), pp. xli ff.

end of the coffin, while people thrice repeat the Pali verse as follows: "Buddham saranam gakkhāmi, Dhamman saranam gakkhāmi, Samgham saranam gakkhāmi" ("I take my refuge in Buddha, I take my refuge in Dhamma, and I take my refuge in Order." [4] Following this, the monk responds thrice, repeating the well-known verse in Pali: "Anikkā vata samkhārā uppādavayadhammino, Uppaggitvā nirugghanti tesam vūpasamo sukho" ("How transient are all component things! Their nature is to be born and die; coming, they go; and then is best, when each has ceased, and all is rest").[5] After this, they pour some water into a cup, until the cup is full to the brim, and chant three times another Pali verse in blessing of the departed one. The coffin is then put into the grave, and each throws in a handful of earth. After the ceremony is over, a feast follows. Cremation is also prevalent, with a long complex ceremony. After the body is burned, ashes are collected and preserved in stupas of monasters. There are special stupas built only for preservation of relics of high-ranked monks or laymen.

Though cremation also prevailed in China, the rites were influenced by Chinese tradition, especially amongst the Ch'an monks. When an abbot dies, his corpse is bathed and clothed, and the head shaved. The body is placed in its bedroom for one night to enable his followers to pay last respects to the departed master. On the second night, the body is enshrined with a grand ceremony in which his last sermon is intoned. His disciple acts as the chief mourner and a senior monk of the monastery conducts the ceremony. After reading the scriptures and performing worship, the audience is allowed to wail and weep. People then step forward to offer incense according to the order of their position. Tea is offered to the departed master before the assembly is dispersed. On the third day, the shrine containing the body is formally removed to a lecturing hall, and then carried out from the monastery. When the shrine has reached the main gate of the monastery, a sacrificial ceremony takes place. The

[4] *Idem*, p. xlvii.
[5] *Idem*.

chief monk of the monastery stands in front of the shrine and recites holy names and incantations. The shrine and the body are sent to the cremation ground; disciples and friends of the dead attend the ceremony until the body is consumed by fire. Ashes are collected and taken back to the bedroom of the late monk. A ceremony, with the recitation of scriptures and offerings, is again performed. Finally, the ashes are removed into a pagoda and enshrined within it.[6] Of course, this funeral rite cannot be regarded as the only prescription. There were monks who were buried by their disciples or cast into a forest among other methods. But those cases are, however, not common.

Two of the incantations read by Chinese Buddhists in funerals are very popular. One is *Wang-sheng-chou* (incantation for re-birth to the Buddhist paradise); the other, *Leng-yen-chou*, is an extract from the Chinese translation of *Mahāpratyangirādhāraṇī*. It is claimed that the former has the power of helping the dead in future birth; the latter supposedly frees him from heresy and difficulties, and thus assists him to attain enlightenment and to be reborn in the Pureland. It is also beneficial to his descendants and for harvest. Apart from these distinctive worldly inclinations, there are other important features that the Chinese Ch'an Buddhists have written into their funeral regulations in their books of monastic discipline, unlike many of their colleagues of other schools, who depend on unwritten conventions.

In Tibet, the high lamas prefer to be cremated. Corpses of poor families are simply thrown into rivers, and those who died of infections are buried. But the most popular funeral in the land is a gruesome one. After a person has passed away, his family first consults an astrologer for the horoscope. Lamas are invited to read the scriptures and the corpse is kept in the house for 49 days. During this time, food is offered three times daily. The Tibetans believe that the soul departs from the body completely within 49 days. So the corpse is then stripped, the spine broken in two and the body doubled up with the head placed between the knees; it is bound with white cloth and placed in a corner

[6] *Taishu shinshu daizokyo, op. cit.* n. 2025, pp. 1127ff.

of a room, with a cloth curtain separating it from visitors. Butter lamps and offerings are put in front of the curtain and lamas chant prayers incessantly day and night. When these prayers are finished, the personal spiritual teacher of the departed, a lama, cuts the corpse into pieces and scatters them in an accepted spot to feed the birds.[7]

Before concluding this sketch, it is clear that the funeral rite of the Buddhist world uses cremation as the main practice. This is based on the Buddhist teachings that the human body is merely a compound of the four elements of earth, water, fire and air. It is destined to return to those elements. As the doctrine states, impermanence is the nature of life; it is inevitable and one cannot avoid it by whatever means. Therefore the Buddhists are able to control their sorrow caused by death. Regarding the problem of rebirth, it is not mentioned in the Hīnayāna school, but it is constantly featured in the funeral rites of the Mahāyāna Buddhists, though the rebirth may not be materially in this world. Apart from this main principle, the rite has been remarkably changed or modified by local traditions of various countries where Buddhism has spread during later periods. These modifications not only are related in the duration of the rite and the method of disposing of the body, but also reflect various aspects of the custom. Of course, this divergence between religious ideal and institution is not uncommon to the students of religious history.

----◆-◆◎◗-◆----

JAPANESE BUDDHISM AND CREMATION

Kazuo Suitsu, Bofu-Yamaguchi-Ken, Japan

Among the various branches into which the great Buddhist religion divides is that of *Joodo Shinshuu Honganji*, very wide-

[7] T. L. Shen *et al.*, *Tibet and the Tibetans* (Stanford, 1953), pp. 149ff.

spread and of great antiquity in Japan; its founder was *Kenshin Taishi Shinran Shoonin.*

Its object of worship is *Amida Nyoorai* (*"Namuamidabutsu"*). Its doctrine is a simplification of that of Buddhism. Believers, calling on this name of *Namuamidabutsu,* are certain that they are under the protection of this higher Being and that they will after death be transformed into *Hotoke,* this higher Being who achieved beatitude by his deep penetration into Truth; thus they are assured of attaining the enjoyment of both temporal and eternal happiness. And with their minds constantly set on the thought of this reward, they live in the service of this world and of all other men.

This doctrine's ideal is that believers, united among themselves by the same enjoyment of earthly happiness and the same faith, should strive unceasingly to do good in both word and deed, to obey the laws both of natural morality and of civil authority, and to labor in unison for the spreading of the faith. Furthermore they are bound to avoid all reliance on superstitious practices such as divination, etc.

The Funeral Rites of Joodo Shinshuu

This ceremony is composed of a number of distinct actions and is considered, among all the acts of human life, that of transcendent significance; it is therefore performed with great solemnity.

The essential purpose of these actions consists not so much in prayer as such and the offering of intercession for the dead person as in the establishing, by this most solemnly offered intercession, of a strong bond of union between the dead person, now transformed into *Hotoke,* and his family and acquaintances. The ceremonies begin at the moment of death and occur in the following order.

1. *The Recitation of the "Amidakyo".* These initial prayers are also called the *Makurakyo* (the prayers at the head of the bed) because they are recited at the moment of death. They and all those which follow are penetrated with the doctrine elab-

orated over long ages by the various representatives of Buddhism.

The *Amidakyo* is a simplified summary of the doctrine of *Shaka Sanzon* (Buddha, d. 600 B.C.) and is, as it were, an exhortation coming from him in the place of his repose: "*Amidabutsu* is merciful and forgiving toward us sinners, and provided we believe what he teaches and call repeatedly upon his name, the god *Amida* protects us in this world and at our death admits us into heaven."

On the altar, which every faithful Buddhist keeps in his house, sweet-smelling branches are placed, the *shikimi* that are offered to the *Hotoke Sama* alone, or else other greenery if they are unobtainable, though always without blossom; if there is any on them, it is picked off.

Yukan is the name of the bowl of hot water, used to purify the body of the dead person; the body is then dressed in a white kimono folded in a way distinct from that of daily wear; the head is turned toward the north and the face covered with a white veil. (This custom of turning the head toward the north is said to arise from the fact that *Oshaka Sama* died with his head in that direction.)

No ornaments or flowers are placed before the dead person, but only a few vigil lights or lanterns (*otomyo*), kept constantly burning in honor of the *Hotoke Sama,* and the *Shookoo Dai* (thurible) in which sticks of incense are burned in uninterrupted succession.

2. *"Otsuya"* (*The Night Watch*). The parents and closest friends of the dead person spend the night at his side, making sure that the lights and incense do not go out. The bonzes and persons less intimately connected withdraw when they judge fit.

3. *"Nookan"* (*The Placing in the Coffin*). On the morning of the day following, which is normally that of the funeral proper, the body which has until now lain on the ground on its *futon,* the equivalent of our mattress, is placed in the coffin by members of the family, The hands are joined and in them is placed a *Juuzu,* a sort of rosary that Buddhists use and which gives out

a sound as they rub it between their hands while repeating their ejaculatory prayer, *"Namu Amidabutsu"*.

They also invariably place in the coffin a piece of paper with this prayer written on it and also some food that the dead person would like or some object he would value. Although the lid is placed on the coffin at this stage, it is not nailed down until the whole rite is completed.

4. *"Shukkan"* (*The Going Forth to the Cremation*). The prayers called *Kisanboge* are then recited. ("The gate of heaven is not shut; it is open for all men forever. . . . That is why prayers are not to call out for it to be opened to us but rather to arouse the soul to faith and the desire to enter swiftly into heaven.")

The coffin is covered with a silver lamé sheet and placed in the center of the room in front of an altar with vigil lights, candlesticks, thurible, crowns made of paper flowers, and other objects. The colors used are white, silver and black. On it is placed also the name of the *Tera* (temple) to which the dead person belonged or that of *Amida* and also that which the dead person received as the distinctive mark of his religion. This last name believers try to receive while living by means of a ceremony through which, they say, the founder gives it to them; if, when they die, this name has not yet been received, the bonze of the *Tera* to which they belong gives it to them.

The culmination of this stage is a ritual farewell banquet, celebrated before the altar by the family together with the dead person's most intimate friends; this is called the *Tachiba No Zen* (banquet of the moment of setting forth).

5. *"Soobagongyoo"* (*The Funeral Ceremony Properly So Called*). This is celebrated sometimes before the cremation and sometimes after it. When the former, it normally takes place at the dead person's home; there is also a widespread custom of having one more intimate celebration at home with members of the family and those closest to the dead person, followed by another more public and solemn one in some *Tera* or public building.

The scale and solemnity of this part increases in proportion with the dead person's rank in society. Bonzes officiate, and it begins, like everything else, with the recitation of *Shooshinge* prayers, repeating more or less the same ideas, and the offering of incense by the bonzes and family, followed by many speeches of condolence and the reading of telegrams; in the speeches, the virtues of the dead person are highly praised and stories of his life are told. The ceremony concludes with a formal greeting made on behalf of the family by a representative, with further recitation of prayers and offering of incense by all present, one by one.

The person presiding over the ceremony draws it to a conclusion with a few words; the coffin, assuming that this is before the cremation, is drawn into the center of the room and its lid removed; the members of the family one by one take their last farewell of the dead person, and the lid is nailed down. Custom demands that they should strike the final blows with a stone and that they should carry the coffin out of the house, and this last not by the door in normal use but by that of the room itself; it is easy to imagine what this involves if one knows the typical construction of Japanese houses; they are almost entirely surrounded with a sort of gallery with sliding glass (or paper) panelled doors.

It is said that this is the way things are done because the dead person will never be returning to his home.

6. *"Hiya"* (*Cremation*). Once again prayers are said and incense offered. As soon as the body is cremated, the bones are collected with the aid of a pair of sticks, one of wood and one of bamboo, and placed in a sort of small water jar. What we call the Adam's apple the Japanese call the *Nodobotoke* (the *hotoke* of the throat, *hotoke* meaning miniature idol or statue; perhaps the fact that it stands out prominently has something to do with it too). This hyoid bone is set on one side and after the lapse of a few days is taken to the *Tera*. The other remains are preserved with deepest respect on the house altar until the day

of burial; this is usually left until some time later, even forty days or more.

This act of placing the remains on the altar is accompanied, like all the other acts of the ceremony, by prayers of deep religious feeling: "Life in this world is like an illusion, death like a wind that blows to cut short the life of man. No man can tell the day on which he must die . . . and on the day when this wind of death bears away a man's life, the mourning of those he loves can win him no return. . . . After this farewell, bones alone remain; there is one and the same transience for all men; there is no distinction of age. That is why all of us, as long beforehand as we can, fix the eyes of our heart on the thing that matters beyond all other things in our life, and call upon the name of *Amida,* the one who in his mercy saves us."

Once the moment of death is over, the neighbors hasten to the house and they make themselves responsible for everything connected with the funeral rites, from telling the relatives, informing the local authorities, the crematorium, the undertaker, etc., to preparing the food needed during the whole period.

Japanese etiquette demands that, in gratitude for all this, a banquet should be given for them after the conclusion of the ceremonies.

Other funeral customs exist, varying from region to region, above all in the villages—for example, that of placing at the head of the dead person's bed the bowl he used for rice, full of cooked rice and with his chopsticks standing in it vertically, or that of breaking all the crockery he used to use, or that of making an *Okuribi* (fire of farewell) bonfire at the door of the house, burning special branches. But none of these things have any religious foundation and would really be worth suppressing as incompatible with the authentic Buddhist spirit.

Nowadays for most Japanese these ceremonies with their profoundly religious motivation are no more than a custom that has to be followed, sometimes a tiresome one at that by reason of the demands made by etiquette; but both in themselves and in

the way they are performed, these rites show the refinement of
the Japanese soul.

JEWISH BURIAL RITES AND CUSTOMS

R. J. Zwi Werblowsky, Jerusalem, Israel

Since the ordinances of Gamaliel II (2nd century) the Jewish
burial has remained very simple everywhere. The rites and customs in use at such a burial go back to those already mentioned
in the Bible. Moreover, many of these customs are universally
human, such as the closing of the eyes (cf. Gen. 46, 4; Tob. 14,
15), or Semitic, such as the dressing of the dead and the funeral
meal (cf. Jer. 14, 5–8; Ez. 32, 27; 1 Sam. 28, 14). The "be-
wailing" of the dead is as important as the burial itself. For a
dead person not to be bewailed or buried is considered the most
severe punishment one can inflict on anybody, and even crimi-
nals must be spared that penalty (Deut. 21, 22f.; Jer. 7, 33;
Ez. 29, 5; Ps. 79, 3). Some Semitic customs are prohibited
because they are too intimately connected with the pagan cult
of the dead (Lev. 19, 28; Deut. 16, 1). Embalming is mentioned
very exceptionally (Jacob and Joseph in Gen. 50, 2f.; cf. Is. 22,
17). Cremation is only known as a punishment (Gen. 38, 24;
Lev. 20, 14). That the dead person was buried on the day of
dying (Deut. 21, 23) is easily understandable, given the conditions of the climate. Although post-biblical Judaism has preserved many of these biblical customs, late developments have
brought about some modifications. At the approach of death
there is a confession of sins and a confession of faith, and this
confession of faith is recited together with all present. Once
death has taken place, the body is put on the ground and those
that keep vigil with it like to recite Psalm 91. The body is washed

reverently according to the ritual and then wrapped in a simple white cloth. All the servicing connected with the washing and the placing on the bier is done by volunteers or by members of the so-called sacred fraternities. This service, as well as assisting at the funeral and consoling the bereaved, is considered a meritorious deed of brotherly love. The body is put onto the bier in its full length, and is buried in a simple wooden coffin or just put into the grave as it is, while the grave is marked by a stone slab. The burial service consists of psalms, the acceptance of the justice of God's will, a funeral speech in praise of the defunct person, and prayers for the rest of his soul and in praise of God's holy name. Those present spread some soil into the grave and then stand in two rows to make a path for the relatives as they leave the cemetery.

When they have returned from the cemetery friends and neighbors offer the bereaved a simple meal. The next-of-kin put on mourning and stay at home for seven days (cf. 1 Sam. 31, 13), seated on low small chairs. As they must not leave the house, the morning and evening services may be held at home, and there is no need to go to the synagogue. The mourning period varies according to the degree of affinity, and is longest for the death of parents. This mourning period is divided into various sections—the first seven days, the first month, the first year after death—in order to allow those who are left behind to return gradually to normal life. These periods correspond to the phases through which the soul must pass in order to reach the peace of heaven. The mystical theology of the Jewish Kabbala, particularly during the 16th century, spread the conviction that those departed could benefit by the prayers and good works of the living.

The anniversary is marked by relatives reciting prayers and visiting the synagogue. Perhaps the most striking element of Jewish burial customs is the strict insistence on equality in the rites for rich and poor.

A MARXIST VIEW OF BURIAL

Gilbert Mury, Nantèrre, France

A man dies. Those who worked or lived with him gather together. Why should there be a ceremony? Why not simply leave this deserted body alone? The question can be put to a materialist as well as to a Christian. And when one thinks of the fact that neither prayer nor the celebration of the Mass demands in principle that the mortal remains be present, both the Christian and the materialist might give the same answer. To put things more simply, what am I, as a Marxist, conscious of when I take part in this ceremony?

The presence of the body signifies something painful that I can analyze. It shows, through the disappearance of personal consciousness, the absurd character—in the most negative and aggressive sense of the word—of those natural processes out of which man emerges. If being, matter, precedes our actions, which is the meaning we give to the world, then being has no meaning, no aim, no end. Birth, life and death are all part of the same blind necessity. Man, who creates meaning, has only one link with nature: he fights it. The whole of civilization, with all its technique and organization, plays a positive part when it subdues matter, and only then. Among the struggles in which mankind is involved, we must therefore count the attempt to push back death. The earth of the future will not merely bristle with ports for space ships, but with hospitals and laboratories.

And so the presence of the body bears witness to the fact that, within us and outside of us, the battle between us and nature continues. The grief that besets us needs this scandal: a human shape that cannot act and therefore cannot feel. This incoherent appeal, addressed to the dead body, in the hope that it may somehow respond to our caresses and our words, while nobody believes in the miracle of the resurrection, shows precisely that refusal to admit the absolute evil, the material compulsion of being which escapes control by man. We can only understand what we make, therefore a "working" world in which man's hands mold things, where a carpenter makes a table with wood. That is the world of freedom.

Can we understand a world in the opposite sense, a world where things undo man? We can, of course, look for the causes of such a process. But, and this is the essence of the matter, we are incapable of accepting this situation. We are not treating the dead body as a living person, but, confronted with the body, we bear witness that not the whole of man has been destroyed.

The end to personal consciousness is something intolerable. But we do not say this as an existentialist would: for us, consciousness means action. It becomes real in what it does. That is why all is not abolished. The table survives the carpenter and the "job" survives the laborer. Faced with the crushing experience of death, we not merely bear witness but gather together in order to continue what has been undertaken. There are men, according to our Chinese comrades, whose death weighs less than a feather. They are those whose activity is cut off from the future, those that leave nothing to carry on with, those that leave nothing behind because they lived "alone", for themselves, on the fringe of the community, or, worse, in opposition to the community. Those who exploit and their accomplices die completely.

The death of others weighs more heavily than a mountain. This is the death, obviously, of militant revolutionaries, but not exclusively. One may fall on the battlefield or give one's life, quietly, day by day, constantly learning how to put the others above oneself. The peasant of the Middle Ages (of every kind) continues in the child he has fed, in the rural community in which his labor integrated him, in those who continue his labor on the same soil.

That is why the death of a man gathers around his body all those that have lived, worked and fought by his side, in a monotonous and solemn protest.

The meaning of this gathering is clear when the struggling

conscience of a dead person has reached the stage of a clear consciousness of the aims of his struggle. Here we pass from gestures, sentiments and feelings to a higher level of theoretical and practical lucidity. Nevertheless, a hero who has fallen on the battlefield need not necessarily have "lived" anything else than a burning solidarity with the masses of his class, his people, his country; nor is it necessary for an ordinary man to have worked out an intellectual analysis of the "how" he came to prefer the others to himself, or the "we" to his "I", or mutual support to surrender, before he can claim effectively that his life has meaning.

If we have to philosophize about death, let us say once more that parents, friends and comrades protest against the divorce between meaning and being, and that they bear witness by their presence to the continuity of mankind which will revenge itself for the death of the individual on the nature from which the human race has emerged. And since it is the characteristic property of mankind to build up its own history, it is clear that one cannot separate its continuity from the perspective opened up by those collective struggles where not all men or all classes are on the side of man. Sometimes consciously, but more often without realizing it, to bury one's dead is to integrate one's grief in a movement which passes beyond that grief.

And if all this sounds rather trite, the reason is that death itself is a trite tragedy. And even to say this is in itself trite.

◆━◆▶◆━◆

Mortuary Science

Concilium General Secretariat, Nijmegen, Netherlands

As Jessica Mitford suggests in the title of her well-known book,[1] the Americans have invented a "way of death" that cor-

---

[1] J. Mitford, *The American Way of Death* (New York, 1963). A spe-

responds to their "way of life". In the United States death has been "civilized". It has been disentangled from religious anxieties and firmly placed in the atmosphere of modern society. This means, in fact, that the whole equipment of modern techniques and economics is used in order to prevent the reality of death from leaving any traces in the society of the living.

Both in the United States and in England a new word has been coined for what one might call a secularized funeral rite: mortuary science. The name is clever. It might suggest a new branch of science seriously concerned with man's death and its humanization. In fact, it is principally concerned with the surviving relatives of the defunct person. It might be called a science in the sense that the exploiters of this modern funeral rite have, by means of a popular kind of science, succeeded in cataloguing and using the various emotional conditions of the relatives at the moment when death has deprived them of a loved one.

The whole machinery of modern commercialism is discreetly manipulated in order to make the most of these emotional situations for profit. These people look for the most effective means of stripping these emotional situations of such painful and irritating elements as grief, guilt consciousness and inner disturbances. All that is repellent in the presence of the dead is expertly camouflaged, and it is suggested that the defunct person is still there, outwardly presented in the condition in which his relatives prefer to see him. In order to eliminate the painful aspect they deliberately use a scientific term, taken from psychiatry: "therapy": the survivor is effectively cured of his grief by an expert arrangement of environment and atmosphere and a fitting presentation of the earthly remains. "Death can be a happy event on condition that it is allowed to take place in a suitably aesthetic manner." The instinctive wishes of the relatives are analyzed and sublimated in order to sell them the corresponding remedy as

cial chapter is devoted to the situation in England (pp. 202–21) which, according to the Americans, is fifty years behind the modern style of burial in the United States. Evelyn Waugh satirized this style in his *The Loved One.*

dearly as possible. It is a strange mixture of sentiment and businesslike procedure, sufficiently opportunist not to offend any possible religious conviction.

The whole process is based on the emotional vulnerability of the mourners who remain behind and wish to go back to ordinary life as soon as possible. The vulnerability of the surviving relative is the more easily played upon as he is in a state of emotional disturbance. The process appeals to his vanity by manipulating the status symbol, and to his desire to see the defunct live on in history as a famous man. The sense of well-being, stimulated by comfort, a sense of continuity and security in life, is deliberately transferred to the dead person and the coffin in which he is put to rest. The "living standard" is consciously used to push up the "dying standard".

Burying has become a profession which presupposes a whole range of technical qualifications, including such treatment as embalming and application of make-up, which turn the dead body into a "beautiful memory picture" which allows a scientific exploitation of the feelings that beset the relatives at the death of a loved one. The whole process crawls with euphemisms for words like corpse, bier, burying, funeral procession and cemetery, in order to hide the repellent and brutal reality of death: "Every symbol capable of provoking grief in any way must be banned from cemeteries laid out as an earthly paradise; instead, loudspeakers must constantly pour out music and inspiring messages" (H. Eaton, the creator of American cemeteries laid out like pleasure-gardens).

And so consolation has become a viable commercial article. It is no longer that "primitive" expression of sympathy and human sharing, but something professionally produced and for sale. Just as the care of the sick is no longer left to the pity of one's fellowmen, beset with the same human misery, but has become an honorable profession with high ethical standards and scientific training, so the burial of the dead has been taken out of the sphere of privacy and humanity and transferred to the neutral sector of economics and hard business. To be an undertaker is a full-time career, demanding an officially recognized training and diploma. In the United States there is one undertaker for every 7,000 people; in England 1 for every 11,000. This businesslike approach tends to prompt in the relatives needs and requirements which do not really exist, following the pattern of indirect advertising. Training takes place in special colleges, such as the well-known San Francisco College of Mortuary Science. It remains curious that the libraries and numerous periodicals of such institutes are surrounded with an air of secrecy and are in fact only accessible to those undertakers who belong to the Union of Mortuary Management. These undertakers have thus succeeded in turning the style of burial expertly into a status symbol.

And so a new myth is deliberately fostered which is essentially more primitive than, for instance, the myths which surrounded the burial rites of the Incas. The growth of this myth is frankly stimulated in order to justify the high expenses of such a burial. The burial experts themselves believe in this myth and obviously have to in order to maintain themselves in this bizarre occupation. This myth rests on three pillars. The first is that this style of burial is in the American tradition. But this tradition has been artificially created over the last twenty years. The second is the conviction that this burial industry gives the Americans what they want, while, in fact, only those "wants" are cultivated or excessively stimulated which are psychologically most vulnerable: man's vanity, his guilt complex and the emotional disturbance when he is already upset. The third is the agglomeration of half-digested theories of a certain popular psychiatry: grief needs therapy. So they talk of "the dramaturgic role, in which the undertaker becomes a stage manager to create an appropriate atmosphere and to move the funeral party through a drama in which social relationships are stressed and an emotional catharsis or release is provided through ceremony".[2]

Sometimes this whole process has rightly been called "necrolatry"—the worship of the dead. It is a secularized form of super-

2 *Op. cit.*, p. 18.

stition which makes the serious American far from happy and against which he rebels today, even if only because he resents the economic exploitation. In her book, *The American Way of Death*, Jessica Mitford, wife of a member of the Bay Area Funeral Society, has suggested that the present rebellion against this pressure group of undertakers might be related to the growing maturity of American self-awareness: they no longer want to be told what they want but want to decide for themselves in their genuine need of human consolation when faced with the ruthlessness and incomprehensibility of man's death.

———————◆◄◉►◆———————

GENERAL CONCLUSION

Burial rites and customs are as general as death itself. They vary according to man's awareness of the mystery of life. They will therefore differ according to whether this man is primitive, or religious, or wholly secularized, but they all have something in common. It is therefore possible to compare the values of these customs, rites and legislation concerned with burial: they all are a conscious expression of man's attitude toward death. In a very general way they are an expression of protest against death as something that ought not to be, something that is incomprehensible. One may reduce this process to the biological law of self-preservation and fear of death, but this is only one aspect. The rites show just as much, sometimes hopelessly and pathetically, that man refuses to accept a total end. Particularly in the case of Christianity, these rites also show a positive integration of death into man's life. Death is the privileged time and place where living man becomes aware of himself. The most appropriate burial rite would be a rite which would purge this process from illusions and fill it with the reality of life in faith. Death creates confusion in the social environment of the defunct —there is an empty place, change in ownership, someone becomes a widow, etc.—but this milieu must be restored through his faith in the true values and validity of this life that proved so fragile, and this implies also a faith in the Christian values of this life.

Existing burial rites must always be interpreted psychologically and socially, but can never be reduced to mere psychological and social values, not even those of religious psychology. They constitute a true function in the life of those who survive, and this at every level of this life: biological, psychological, religious, Christian, social. A true reform of the burial rite cannot be based on only one of these aspects but should always be related to all the others. At all these levels the rite must express a protest and an attempt at integrating death into life. "Mortuary Science", in particular, has completely eliminated this aspect: it deliberately and expertly hides the reality of death and so deprives the living of a valuable moment of self-awareness. When we see man as a developing consciousness, such a treatment of death really diminishes what is human in us, and therefore what is Christian. Religions may be inclined to be too lenient toward man's illusions. A renewal of the Christian burial rite, too, must free man from many illusions. A genuine renewal of this rite cannot rest satisfied with a few pragmatic adjustments but must take into account what the sciences concerned with man have discovered. The Christian awareness of the mystery of human life does not make growing insights into other levels of life superfluous; it rather presupposes them. Only then can the Christian vision be given an appeal in a burial rite that rounds off the whole of life.

BIOGRAPHICAL NOTES

WILHELM BREUNING: Born in 1920 in Germany, he was ordained in 1948. He studied at the Faculty of Theology of Trier and the University of Bonn, earning his doctorate in theology in 1954 and his lectorate in dogmatic theology in 1958. He has been professor of dogmatic theology at the Faculty of Theology of Trier since 1960. His publications include *Die hypostatische Union in der Theologie Wilhelms von Auxerre, Hugos von St. Cher und Rolands von Cremona* (1962) and he is a contributor to *Trierer Theologische Zeitschrift*.

JORDI PINELL PONS, O.S.B.: Born in 1921 in Barcelona, Spain, he was ordained in 1953. He studied at the University of Louvain and in Rome at the Gregorian and at the Faculty of Theology of St. Anselmo, earning his doctorate in theology in 1966. He is currently professor of liturgy at St. Anselmo and advisor to the Consilium of the *Constitution on the Sacred Liturgy*. Among his books are *Los Textos de la antigua liturgía hispánica* (Toledo, 1965) and *Las horas vigiliares del oficio monacal hispánico* (Monserrat, 1966). He is a frequent contributor to such publications as *Archivos Leoneses* and *Hispanía Sacra*.

WILLIAM F. MACOMBER, S.J.: Born in Massachusetts, he was ordained in 1956. He studied at Harvard University and Weston College and at the Pontifical Institute for Oriental Studies in Rome. He gained degrees in philosophy and theology, earning his doctorate in Oriental studies, and has been professor of Oriental liturgy at the Pontifical Institute for Oriental Studies since 1964. His publications include two articles in *Orientalia Christiana Periodica:* "The Theological Synthesis of Cyrus of Edessa" (1964) and "The Oldest Known Text of the Anaphora of the Apostles Addai and Mari" (1966).

DAMIEN SICARD: Born in France in 1925, he was ordained in 1948. He studied at the Major Seminary of Montpellier and the Catholic Institute of Lyons, gaining his degree in theology. He is professor at the Major Seminary and vicar apostolic of Montpellier. His publications include *La prédication en station balnéaire* (1954) and "Le décret conciliaire 'Ad Gentes'," in *Mission de l'Eglise* (June, 1967).

ANTONIO SAVIOLI: Born in 1915 in Italy, he was ordained in 1940. He studied at the Architectural Faculty of the University of Florence, gaining his doctorate in 1966. He is professor of the history of art at the Pius XII Seminary of Ravenna, and advisor to the International Museum of Ceramics at Faenza. He is a contributor to *Chiesa e Quartiere et Quaderni della Cattedrale di Faenza* and *L'Osservatore Romano*.

† THEODOR FILTHAUT: The Secretariat of *Concilium* received the manuscript of Professor Theodor Filthaut's article and the news of his death almost simultaneously. He was born in 1907 at Duisburg, Germany, and died on October 31, 1967. He gained his doctorate and lectorate in theology, and held the post of professor of pastoral theology at the Catholic Faculty of Theology at Münster University from 1957 until his death. His most recent publication was *Zeichen der Auferstehung Zur Erneuerung der christlichen Grabkunst* (1965); he is also the author of *Learning to Worship* (London, 1966). He was a member of the editorial board of the review *Diaconia*.

LADISLAUS BOROS, S.J.: Born in Budapest in 1927, he was ordained in 1957. He attended Jesuit houses of study in Hungary, Austria, Italy and France, and also the University of Munich, where he received his doctorate in philosophy. He is dean of studies of philosophy and religion in the Theological Faculty of the University of Innsbruck. His published works include *The Moment of Truth* (London & New York, 1965), *God Is with Us* (London & New York, 1967) and *Pain and Providence* (London & Baltimore, 1967).

LUIS MALDONADO: Born in Spain, he was ordained in 1954. He studied at the universities of Comillas and Salamanca in Spain, and at the universities of Innsbruck, Austria and Freiburg im Breisgau in Germany, gaining his degree in philosophy and a doctorate in theology. Since 1962 he has been professor of liturgy at the Institute of Pastoral Studies at the University of Salamanca. His publications include *La plegaría eucarística* (1967) and *El Mensaje de los Cristianos* (1965).

THEODORE STONE: Born in Chicago in 1926, he was ordained in 1952. He studied in the United States, gaining his degrees in the arts and theology. He is archdiocesan director for the Chicago Center of the Confraternity of Christian Doctrine, and a member of the subcommittee for the adaptation of the liturgy. His published works include *Pastoral Catechetics* (1964) and *World* (1967).

SISTER ANSELM CUNNINGHAM, O.P.: Born in Milwaukee in 1936, she studied at Rosary College and at the universities of Illinois and Loyola, gaining her M.A. She is responsible for research and coordination of the religious education syllabus in the archdiocese of Chicago.

HEINRICH RENNINGS: Born in Moers, Germany in 1926, he was ordained for the diocese of Münster in 1955. After studying at Innsbruck and Münster, and at the Institut supérieur de Liturgie in Paris, he received a doctorate in philosophy in 1952 and a doctorate in theology in 1965. He has been an instructor in liturgy at Trier and has also been active in the Liturgical Institute there. He is editor of the series *Lebendiger Gottesdienst* started in Münster in 1961.

HELMUT HUCKE: Born in Kassel, Germany in 1927, he studied at the Musikhochschule and at the University of Freiburg im Breisgau, where he earned his doctorate. He is editor of the *Neuen Psalmenbuch,* co-editor of the review *Musik und Altar,* assistant at the Musicological Institute of the University of Frankfurt and head of the musical department of the German Historical Institute in Rome. He is the author of several important articles in musicology.

JACOBUS THEUWS, O.F.M.: Born in Belgium in 1914, he studied at Louvain, at the Witwatersrand University of Johannesburg, South Africa, and at the Institute of Social Anthropology at Oxford where he gained his doctorate in philosophy and literature in 1953. Since 1966 he has been professor at the University of Lubumbashi in Congo-Kinshasa. His published works include *De Afrikaanse Mens en zijn Cultuur* in collaboration with Burssens and Jacoby (1966) and "Rites et Religion en Afrique," in *Revue du Clergé africain* (May, 1965).

ALBERT NADER: Born in Egypt in 1911, he studied at the Faculty of Literature of the Sorbonne, gaining his doctorate in the philosophy of literature in 1949. Since 1955 he has taught at the University of the Lebanon and at the Institute of Oriental Studies in Beirut. His many writings include "Les courants d'idées en Islam," a series of articles published in the Beirut paper *L'Orient* (1959), and "Le 'Logos' dans le pensée musulmane," in *Revue de la Société de Philosophie du Maroc* (1967).

QUDRATULLAH HAFIZ: Born in 1917, he is a Mohammedan from West Pakistan. He obtained degrees in Arabian literature and theology at Punjab University, and is imam of his co-religionists in the Netherlands. His published works include *De grondslagen van de Islam* (1950). He is a frequent contributor to the reviews *Al-Islam* (The Netherlands) and *Al Fazl* (Pakistan).

CYRIL PAPALI, O.C.D.: Born in India in 1902, he studied in India, and is professor of Indology and missiology at the Teresianum and Universitas Urbaniana. His publications include *Hinduismus,* 2 vols. (1953 & 1960) and "The Place of Non-Christian Religions in the Economy of Salvation," in *Seminarium* 1 (1967).

LOUIS WEI TSING-SING: Born in Shanghai in 1903, he was ordained in 1966. He was a journalist and attaché at the Chinese Embassy in Paris from 1947 to 1953. His many publications include his doctoral thesis *La Politique missionaire de la France en Chine 1842–1856. L'Ouverture des cinq ports chinois au commerce étranger et liberté religieuses* (1961). He is a frequent contributor to the *Revue d'Histoire Ecclésiastique* (Louvain).

JAN YÜN-HUA: Born in China in 1924, he is a Buddhist. He is assistant professor of religion at McMaster University in Hamilton, Canada. His publications include *Buddhist Historiography in Sung China* (1964) and *Buddhist Relations between India and Sung China* (1966).

KAZUO SUITSU: Born in Japan in 1927, he is a Jodoshinshu Buddhist. He studied medicine at the University of Osaka, gaining his doctorate in 1959. He is a psychiatrist and member of the Japanese Medical Association. He has contributed important articles to Japanese medical reviews.

R. J. ZWI WERBLOWSKY: Born in Germany in 1924, he is a Jewish rabbi. He studied in London and Geneva, where he gained his doctorate in literature. He is professor of comparative religions at the Faculty of Humanities at the Hebrew University of Jerusalem, and has been dean of that Faculty since 1965. His published works include *Lucifer et Prométhée* (1951).

GILBERT MURY: Born in Paris in 1920, he studied at the Faculty of Literature in Bordeaux and Paris. He was formerly a reporter for the Communist press and secretary-general of the Bureau of Marxist Study and Research. His publications include *Les classes sociales en France* (1963) and *Christianisme primitif et morale moderne* (1960).